How to Be Happy
According to Jesus

The Beatitudes

Matthew 5:1–12

Dr. David Jeremiah

Turning Point
with Dr. David Jeremiah

© 1996, 2004 by Turning Point for God
P.O. Box 3838
San Diego, CA 92163
All Rights Reserved

Unless otherwise indicated, Scripture verses quoted are taken from the NEW KING JAMES VERSION.

Printed in the United States of America.

Contents

About Dr. David Jeremiah and Turning Point . . 4

About This Study Guide 5

Introduction 7

1. Life Outside the Amusement Park
   Matthew 5:1–12 9

2. Happy Are the Humble
   Matthew 5:3 21

3. Happy Are the Hurting
   Matthew 5:4 33

4. Happy Are the Harnessed
   Matthew 5:5 45

5. Happy Are the Hungry
   Matthew 5:6 57

6. Happy Are the Helpers
   Matthew 5:7 67

7. Happy Are the Holy
   Matthew 5:8 79

8. Happy Are the Healers
   Matthew 5:9 91

9. Happy Are the Harassed
   Matthew 5:10–12 103

10. How to Really Be Happy
    Matthew 5:1–12 115

Resources 126

Price List 128

About Dr. David Jeremiah and Turning Point

Dr. David Jeremiah is the founder of Turning Point, a ministry committed to providing Christians with sound Bible teaching relevant to today's changing times through radio and television broadcasts, audio series, and books. Dr. Jeremiah's common-sense teaching on topics such as family, prayer, worship, angels, and biblical prophecy forms the foundation of Turning Point.

David and his wife, Donna, reside in El Cajon, California, where he is the senior pastor of Shadow Mountain Community Church and chancellor of Christian Heritage College. David and Donna have four children and six grandchildren.

In 1982, Dr. Jeremiah brought the same solid teaching to San Diego television that he shares weekly with his congregation. Shortly thereafter, Turning Point expanded its ministry to radio. Dr. Jeremiah's inspiring messages can now be heard on radio and television nationally and internationally.

Because Dr. Jeremiah desires to know his listening audience, he travels nationwide holding "A Night of Encouragement" ministry rallies and Spiritual Enrichment conferences that touch the hearts and lives of many. According to Dr. Jeremiah, "At some point in time, everyone reaches a turning point; and for every person, that moment is unique, an experience to hold onto forever. There's so much changing in today's world that sometimes it's difficult to choose the right path. Turning Point offers people an understanding of God's Word as well as the opportunity to make a difference in their lives."

Dr. Jeremiah has authored numerous books, including *Escape the Coming Night* (Revelation), *The Handwriting on the Wall* (Daniel), *Overcoming Loneliness, What the Bible Says About Angels, The Power of Encouragement, Prayer—The Great Adventure, God in You* (Holy Spirit), *Gifts from God* (Parenting), *Jesus' Final Warning, When Your World Falls Apart, Slaying the Giants in Your Life, My Heart's Desire, Sanctuary, The Things That Matter, Life Wide Open, The Prayer Matrix,* and *Searching for Heaven on Earth.*

About This Study Guide

The purpose of this Turning Point study guide is to reinforce Dr. David Jeremiah's dynamic, in-depth teaching on the Beatitudes, and to aid the reader in applying biblical truth to his or her daily life. This study guide is designed to be used in conjunction with Dr. Jeremiah's *How to Be Happy According to Jesus* audio series, but it may also be used by itself for personal or group Bible study.

Structure of the Lessons

Each lesson is based on one of the messages in the *How to Be Happy According to Jesus* audiocassette or compact disc series and focuses on a specific passage in the book of Matthew. Each lesson is composed of the following elements:

- *Outline*

The outline at the beginning of the lesson gives a clear, concise picture of the passage being studied and provides a helpful framework for readers as they listen to Dr. Jeremiah's teaching.

- *Overview*

The overview summarizes Dr. Jeremiah's teaching on the passage being studied in the lesson. Readers should refer to the biblical passages in their own Bibles as they study the overview.

- *Application*

This section contains a variety of questions designed to help readers dig deeper into the lesson and the Scriptures, and to apply the lesson to their daily lives. For Bible study groups or Sunday school classes, these questions will provide a springboard for group discussion and interaction.

- *Did You Know?*

This section presents a fascinating fact, historical note, or insight that adds a point of interest to the preceding lesson.

Using This Guide for Group Study

The lessons in this study guide are suitable for Sunday school classes, small-group studies, elective Bible studies, or home Bible study groups. Each person in the group should have his or her own study guide.

When possible, the study guide should be used with the corresponding tape or compact disc series. You may wish to assign the study guide as homework prior to the meeting of the group and then use the meeting time to listen to the tape and discuss the lesson.

FOR CONTINUING STUDY

A complete catalog of Dr. Jeremiah's materials for personal and group study is available through Turning Point. To obtain a catalog, additional study guides, or more information about Turning Point, call 1-800-947-1993, write to: Turning Point, P.O. Box 3838, San Diego, CA 92163, or go online at turningpointonline.org.

Dr. Jeremiah's *Turning Point* program is currently heard or viewed around the world on radio, television, and the Internet in English. *Momento Decisivo*, the Spanish translation of Dr. Jeremiah's messages, can be heard on radio in every Spanish speaking country in the world. In some areas, the television broadcast provides Arabic subtitles, and in others, it is translated into the Russian language.

Contact Turning Point for radio and television program times and stations in your area, or visit our website at www.turningpointonline.org.

HOW TO BE HAPPY ACCORDING TO JESUS

INTRODUCTION

In the syndicated cartoon "Mister Boffo," cartoonist Joe Martin once drew a middle-aged man lying on a psychologist's couch. The psychologist is sitting on a chair next to the couch, listening intently, and writing in a notebook. The man lying on the couch is speaking: "I drive a Mercedes," he says, "I have a beachhouse in Bermuda, a twelve-room penthouse, a ninety-foot yacht. My clothes are made by the finest tailors in London. I have a world-class wine cellar. And yet I'm still not happy."

The psychologist looks up and asks, "Do you have a Rolex?"

The troubled man abruptly raises his head off the couch, raises a finger in the air, and declares, "Why no, I don't!"

Our world is full, unfortunately, of such folly as this—troubled people thinking they are just one purchase away from true, permanent happiness.

Where did we get the idea that the things of this world were supposed to be a source of happiness for us? Peggy Noonan, former speechwriter for President Ronald Reagan, wrote in a 1992 *Forbes* magazine article that the notion arose a few decades ago: "Somewhere in the seventies, or the sixties, we started expecting to be happy, and changed our lives (left town, left families, switched jobs) if we were not. And society strained and cracked in the storm. I think we have lost the old knowledge that happiness is overrated—that, in a way, life is overrated. We have lost, somehow, a sense of mystery—about us, our purpose, our meaning, our role. Our ancestors believed in two worlds, and understood this to be the solitary, poor, nasty, brutish, and short one. We are the first generation of man that actually expected to find happiness here on earth, and our search for it has caused such unhappiness. The reason: If you do not believe in another higher world, if you believe only in the flat material world around you, if you believe that this is your only chance at happiness—if that is what you believe, then you are not disappointed when the world does not give you a good measure of its riches. You are despairing."

Ms. Noonan has it right. If we expect this world to make us happy, then we have lost what prior generations understood better than we: that we are pilgrims and strangers in this world, just passing through. But that is not to dismiss lightly the statement of Jesus that He came to give us abundant life (John 10:10), or His Beatitudes (the subject of this study) in which happiness appears to be within the grasp of those who possess certain perspectives and characteristics.

Note the difference between this world's version of happiness—sensory pleasure, laughter, frivolity, and the absence of pain—and the Bible's: blessedness, deep-seated fulfillment and wholeness, an eternal perspective that explains the temporal. How blessed, Jesus said, how fulfilled and satisfied are those who . . . .

Who what? Who are poor in spirit, who mourn, who are meek, who seek righteousness, who are merciful, who are pure, who make peace, and who are persecuted for the sake of the kingdom of God. Those are the Beatitudes of Jesus—the descriptions of blessing that attend those who live by the values of the kingdom of God even while they live in this world (Matthew 5:1–12).

Those who look to this world to meet their needs will be doubly disappointed. It can only occasionally provide temporary happiness (by the world's definition) and can never provide permanent fulfillment. The blessedness, fulfillment, and satisfaction that Christ promised in His Beatitudes are the subject of this study guide. How blessed are those who read His words and practice them.

LESSON 1

LIFE OUTSIDE THE AMUSEMENT PARK

Matthew 5:1–12

In this lesson we discover and define the meaning of true happiness.

OUTLINE

There has never been a time in history when mankind has been more entertained and more unhappy at the same time. While entertainment certainly has its place, it cannot replace true happiness. Happiness is a by-product of knowing God, not an end in itself.

I. The Pursuit of True Happiness Is Part of God's Purpose for You and Me

II. The Pursuit of True Happiness Is a Journey Inward

III. The Pursuit of True Happiness Is Not a Goal, but a By-Product

IV. The Pursuit of True Happiness Will Lead You Ultimately to Jesus Christ

OVERVIEW

Leonard Griffith once wrote, "The trouble with you Americans is that you have to be so confoundedly happy. You have dedicated yourselves to the pursuit of happiness. And you boast about it as an inalienable right, as though happiness were the supreme and absolute goal of all existence. Surely there are more important things in life than just to be happy."

Happiness is an American right. It's in our Declaration of Independence, right alongside life and liberty. I know people living within that truth of the Declaration of Independence, their whole life wrapped up in the pursuit of happiness. Sometimes it can be confusing to watch them. One man buys a dozen homes in hopes of making himself happy; another goes into the wilderness to live like a hermit. One woman becomes a nun in hopes of finding happiness, another a harlot. One young man thinks happiness is found in body building, while another tries to find it by destroying his body with drugs. One couple thinks happiness is found in children, while another couple is convinced children get in the way of happiness.

Malcolm Muggeridge once called the pursuit of happiness the most disastrous purpose set before mankind, something slipped into the Declaration after "life and liberty" at the last moment, almost by accident. "Happiness is like a young deer," Muggeridge said, "fleet and beautiful. Hunt him, and he becomes a poor frantic quarry; after the kill, just a piece of stinking flesh." In his *Screwtape Letters*, C. S. Lewis had the arch-devil, Screwtape, advise his apprentice demons on the lure of happiness. He called it "an ever-increasing craving for an ever-diminishing pleasure." That's exactly how the pursuit of happiness works in this world.

In James Houston's book, *In Pursuit of Happiness*, a woman named Gloria describes her pursuit of happiness as being at an amusement park.

> Many times I have felt as if I am trapped on a huge roller coaster that goes up and down, round and round. Sometimes I manage to escape and get off the mad ride, but I'm still in the amusement park. Outside the park the world looks exciting, but it's too risky. I'm not sure that I could survive out there, so the amusement park remains still the biggest attraction in my life. For everyone is being persuaded to

stay inside the gates of the amusement park and get back on the roller coaster . . . Yet I still think of people in the past who have gone outside the park. They are the ones who truly seek God with all their heart, mind, soul, and body, and are fully prepared to give it all up. They are the ones who live uncompromising lives, who don't feel the grip of money, the pressure of society, the weakened desire for goodness, the punctured self-discipline, the crushing fear of the future, the horror of death, the threat of injustice, the need of security, the rule of self. They don't struggle for faith, hope, and love; they pour out from them and through them. It is these people outside the park who seem to be so totally free . . . I am not happy. I wish I could live outside the amusement park. I wish I had the stuff to do it, but I am afraid at the center I am empty.

I know people who live in the amusement park, getting off the roller coaster long enough to gaze through the gates at real life outside, but without the courage to go there. As soon as the roller coaster stops, they get back on. Pleasure is an anesthesia for deadening the pain of their empty lives. There seem to be few happy people around today. That's why I appreciate the words of Jesus in the Sermon on the Mount. Nine different times Jesus uses the word *blessed*, which roughly translates to "happy." The core values Jesus offers in the Beatitudes describe life that is really worth living: life outside the amusement park.

Blessed means "happy, blissful, joyous, ecstatic." In the original Greek, there is no verb in any of the Beatitudes. So the verses literally say, "Blessed the meek" and "Blessed the poor in spirit." Those characteristics the Lord lists are like an explosion on His lips, a description of the inner joy we can experience. This expression was commonly seen in the book of Psalms. "Blessed is the man who walks not in the counsel of the ungodly," it says in Psalm 1:1. Anyone who has ever been burned by ungodly counsel will attest to the fact that a man who doesn't get mixed up with ungodly counsel is happy. "Blessed is he whose transgression is forgiven," we read in Psalm 32:1. We are to be blissful and ecstatic over the fact that the Lord has taken away our sins. That's the same expression Christ used when He began talking about the Christian life. *Blissful, happy, joyous*—these are the words that describe the Christian walk.

Matthew 5:1–12 describes nine characteristics of the happy Christian life. If you want to know what happiness is all about,

Life Outside the Amusement Park • 11

search through this "happiness manifesto" from the Lord Jesus. He'll explain to you what true happiness is all about. As you study them carefully, you'll find some surprising truths becoming clear.

The Pursuit of True Happiness Is Part of God's Purpose for You and Me

C. S. Lewis enjoyed telling the story of the child who was asked what he thought God was like. As far as the child could make out, God was always snooping around to see if anyone was enjoying himself so that He could put a stop to it! Have you ever known anyone like that? There are Christians who act that way—"If you're not sad, you can't be holy." But that's dead wrong. Jesus said in John 10:10 that He came "that they may have life, and that they may have it more abundantly." God's purpose is not to create a joyless existence. Jesus spoke those words to make it clear to us that God wants us to be blessed. It's part of His purpose.

Anyone who sees Jesus in any other light is missing the point of His life. When you read about the winsomeness of Jesus and the way He came, eating and drinking, you'll see that the Lord enjoyed life. He enjoyed the banquets and the gathering of friends in homes. He mingled with publicans and sinners, and He was the kind of man who attracted little children to himself. He had a sense of humor, too, though many people miss it when they read Scripture. He pictured a man with a plank hanging out of his eye, squinting as he removed a speck of sawdust from the eye of a brother. Those who heard that illustration must have giggled with delight at the verbal picture.

The people who try to paint a picture of Jesus as someone sad or morbid have missed the complete picture. He delighted in life, and He wanted us to be happy. He gave us the Beatitudes so we would know how to do it. We all have been touched by legalism, but the people of God should be filled with a radiant joy so contagious it cannot be held in. That is the heart of the Lord for you and me.

The Pursuit of True Happiness Is a Journey Inward

Those who are truly happy will fit the criteria of what Christ says in Matthew chapter five. A quick scan of chapter 5, verses 1–12 reveals thoughts that run contrary to our current ideas about happiness. There isn't one single reference by the Lord to health, work, income, financial security, homes, love, or friends. Christ knew that while these things often accompany happiness, they do not ever produce it. His list completely reverses the standards of the world. "Oh, the bliss of the poor!" says Jesus. "The joy of the persecuted! The exaltation of the hungry and thirsty! The happiness of the sorrowful!" These are contradictions to the world's standards. They are sayings that no man can hear without shock or amazement. They are paradoxes that Jesus used to destroy the foolish illusions that so many of His followers had built up about what would happen when He became king.

His followers wanted dominion and prosperity, and Jesus spoke of poverty and sorrow, cutting right to the heart of the people. The words must have disgusted many who heard them. They were like cold water on the hot enthusiasm that so many had for the kingdom. The people were certain the kingdom was going to make them free and rich, but Jesus said in effect, "That's not what the kingdom is about at all."

The Pursuit of True Happiness Is Not a Goal, but a By-Product

People who start out with the purpose of trying to become happy very seldom arrive at that place. Happiness sought for its own sake is usually self-defeating. The world is on a lark, trying to find new ways to be happy, but what people are really doing is trying to mask the pain temporarily.

I read a quote once from a man who said, "I think I must be the happiest man in the world! I have never met anyone who has had as much fun as I have had." The words were not spoken by a playboy or a globetrotter or an adventurer. They were spoken by a Christian missionary by the name of Frank Laubach, whose life was dedicated to the cultivation of literacy among the backward people of the world. He never went searching for happiness— he just found it as a by-product of his search for something more important. Dr. Laubach described delighted men and women weeping for joy when they discovered how to read. "No other work in the world could possibly have brought me so much happiness," he said. He didn't live with prosperity or worldly success, but he found happiness. True joy is a by-product, not a goal.

THE PURSUIT OF TRUE HAPPINESS WILL LEAD YOU ULTIMATELY TO JESUS CHRIST

The fifth chapter of Matthew records the words of Jesus regarding happiness. He was an extremely happy man, and His inner joy no doubt came partly from relationships. He had a group of friends who loved Him, and He was endowed with the ability to speak and to heal. If you have a ministry, you know what great joy can be derived from it. Yet over time, the ministry of Jesus Christ shrank. Fewer people followed Him until the night of the Last Supper when there were just His twelve disciples close by. Knowing that He was about to die and witness the desertion of even His closest friends, Jesus still was able to tell them, "These things I have spoken to you, that My joy may remain in you, and that your joy may be full" (John 15:11).

Jesus, with everything about to come undone, was still able to tell His disciples that He wanted them to be joyful. Can you imagine a man about to die the most terrible of deaths talking of His joy and gladness? Either He must have been insane, or He had an incredible resource of happiness about which our world knows very little. The verses in Matthew chapter five explain His joy, and His words can change our lives. It may not immediately change the way you outwardly live, but it will help you find the inner peace and happiness that makes it possible to find joy in the midst of trial.

When the business in which you have invested your life savings fails, you can still find joy. When the child in whom you have invested your life turns south instead of north, there will still be gladness. When people begin to reject you and turn against you, you can still find happiness in Him. As we work through this study, may each of us discover the joy of knowing the Lord, having our sins forgiven, being confident that He has a plan for our lives, and that heaven is on the agenda. May we find happiness as we look to the words of Jesus Christ in the Beatitudes.

APPLICATION

1. Read Matthew 5:1–12.

    - Whose is the kingdom of heaven? (verse 3)

    - Who shall be comforted? (verse 4)

    - Who shall inherit the earth? (verse 5)

    - Who will be filled with righteousness? (verse 6)

    - Who will obtain mercy? (verse 7)

    - Who will see God? (verse 8)

    - Who will be called sons of God? (verse 9)

    - To whom else belongs the kingdom of heaven? (verse 10)

    - Who will receive a great reward in heaven? (verses 11–12a)

Life Outside the Amusement Park

2. How would you define the overall message of these words? What does Jesus want His disciples to learn?

   a. What is the context of much of what follows the Sermon on the Mount? (see verse 17)

   b. What similar phrases do you find in the beginning of the following verses?
      - verse 5:21

      - verse 5:27

      - verse 5:31

      - verse 5:33

      - verse 5:38

      - verse 5:43

c. What term of contrast begins the verses following each of the above six verses?

d. What is Jesus' purpose in citing the Law and Jewish traditions and following it with "But?" What contrast is He setting up?

e. How do the character traits in verses 1–12 set the stage for this discussion?

f. What do verses 1–12 focus on—internal or external matters?

g. What do verses 21, 27, 31, 33, 38, and 43 focus on—internal or external matters?

h. Which does Jesus seem to be focusing on—externals or internals?

3. What do the following verses suggest about achieving a state of "blessedness?"

   a. Psalm 1:1

   b. Psalm 32:1–2

   c. Psalm 33:12

   d. Psalm 34:8

   e. Psalm 41:1

   f. Psalm 84:5

   g. Psalm 94:12

   h. Psalm 112:1

i. Obviously "Blessed is/are" was common phraseology in the Old Testament. Why do you think Jesus used that phrase in His new summary of kingdom character?

j. What difference or contrast do you see between the Old Testament means of being blessed and the means for being blessed in Matthew 5:1–12?

4. What contrast do you see between seeking true happiness in Matthew 5:1–12 and seeking happiness in the world?

   a. How would the world describe a person who manifests the characteristics found in Matthew 5:1–12?

   b. Write out a definition of blessedness (true happiness and well-being) according to . . .
      • the world:

      • Matthew 5:1–12

Life Outside the Amusement Park • 19

5. What makes you happy in the sense of "blessedness" (true, deep-seated sense of well-being)?

   a. How has your own understanding of happiness changed since becoming a Christian?

   b. How do you find your definition of happiness changing the older you get?

DID YOU KNOW?

Matthew's gospel has been called a book of discourses since he arranged Jesus' teachings into five lengthy discourses. The Sermon on the Mount (Matthew 5–7) is the first of the five, followed by discourses in chapter 10 (the occasion of the commissioning of the twelve disciples), chapter 13 (a group of parables), chapter 18 (life in the kingdom of God), and chapters 24–25 [the Olivet Discourse (from the Mount of Olives) concerning the end of the age.] Interestingly, Jesus delivered His new kingdom laws on a mountain (Matthew 5:1) just as Moses received the original Law on a mountain (Mount Sinai; Exodus 19:3).

LESSON 2

Happy Are the Humble

Matthew 5:3

In this lesson we learn how a truly humble person lives.

OUTLINE

Imagine a book titled *Humility and How I Achieved It*. That kind of humility is often practiced in modern times: one that is recognized as being a desirable trait but is used solely for the purpose of self-promotion. True humility is about promoting God, not self.

   I. Those Who Are Poor in Spirit Will Recognize That They Are Out of Step with the World

  II. Those Who Are Poor in Spirit Will Realize Their Emptiness Apart from God

 III. Those Who Are Poor in Spirit Will Reach Out to Others with a Spirit of Love and Compassion

  IV. Those Who Are Poor in Spirit Will Respond to Life with a Spirit of Gratitude

   V. Those Who Are Poor in Spirit Will Reach Their Highest Joy in Serving

OVERVIEW

Have you ever noticed how many unhappy people there are in this world? With all the comforts and gadgets of our modern world, we don't seem to have found the key to happiness. Even among Christians, with all the God-given gifts at their disposal, there seems to be a lack of happiness. Peggy Noonan, speechwriter for Presidents Ronald Reagan and George Bush, wrote about our national lack of happiness in her book, *What I Saw at the Revolution*. She mentioned that it is embarrassing to live in the most comfortable time in the history of man and still not be happy. In the 1950s, we all watched Ralph and Alice Kramden get by in a small rented apartment with a table, two chairs, and one bureau standing in front of a faded wall. By the 1990s, the set on *Family Ties* consisted of couches, lamps, VCRs, color TVs, and fancy art on the wall. We have more things than our parents did, but we aren't happy; and we feel defensive about it. The dad in the 1950s worked hard to make ends meet. He might not have been happy; but he wasn't put here to be happy, so the knowledge of his unhappiness didn't weigh on him. In the words of Peggy Noonan, "He looks perhaps to other, more eternal forms of comfort."

But somewhere in the sixties or seventies we started living with the expectation of happiness. People started moving, changing jobs or changing partners in a quest for happiness. As Noonan describes it, "We . . . lost the old knowledge that happiness is overrated." You see, our forebears understood that this is a short, brutal existence we live here on earth to be followed by an eternity with the Lord. But our generation has decided that this time on earth is the only existence we'll have, the only chance at happiness. So if we search and don't find happiness, we are left only with despair. Many people have pitted their hopes on what this world can provide; and when things start to go bad, they have nothing left to bring them joy and peace.

Jesus, in His greatest sermon, spoke to people brutalized and conquered by the Roman armies. They were subdued, poor, and without hope or expectation, yet the Lord said to them, "Happy are the poor in spirit." How could their miserable lives be described as happy?

In the first words of this great sermon, Jesus begins to describe a new kingdom. It is not the outward kingdom where most people seek happiness, but the inward kingdom of the heart. When He speaks of the "poor in spirit," Jesus is not talking about material poverty, but about spiritual pride. He is speaking of the inward attitude of the heart. With nowhere else to turn, the desperate may turn to Jesus, the only One who can offer the deliverance they seek. The poor in spirit have the advantage of being able to cry out to God for help.

A person who is poor in spirit goes begging on the inside. His heart is destitute, and he is begging for God to get to the bottom of his problem. When a person comes to this sense of emptiness, he is on the threshold of happiness through the kingdom of God. Psalm 34:18 says, "The Lord is near to those who have a broken heart, and saves such as have a contrite spirit." David noted that "the sacrifices of God are a broken spirit, a broken and a contrite heart—These, O God, You will not despise" (Psalm 51:17). God identifies with those who beg on the inside.

Jesus once told a story of two men praying in the temple. One, a Pharisee, proudly told God all the wonderful things he had done. The other, a tax collector, humbly beat his breast and muttered, "God, be merciful to me, a sinner!" The Lord told this story to a crowd of people who thought themselves righteous, and He noted that it was the tax collector who went home justified. "For everyone who exalts himself will be humbled, and he who humbles himself will be exalted" (Luke 18:14). That tax collector had money, but in spite of his outward wealth, he had a sense of the bankruptcy of his heart. In his emptiness, he cried out to God for mercy. He was blessed because he found God. The Pharisee couldn't get over his self-righteousness and pride to find God. It was the tax collector who came away joyful and at peace because he had found the Lord. Happiness is an inward thing, not an outward thing. Blessed are the poor in spirit. I wrestle with that concept since our culture tries to equate happiness with material wealth, but there are at least five things that are outward signs of the inward heart.

THOSE WHO ARE POOR IN SPIRIT WILL RECOGNIZE THAT THEY ARE OUT OF STEP WITH THE WORLD

When a famous basketball player retired at the peak of his career, the owner of the team spoke of him "living the American Dream. The dream is to reach a point in your life where you don't have to do anything you don't want to do, and can do everything that you want to do." After he retired, the man found he wasn't so great at other things. So he went back to playing basketball again. Whatever he was searching for, he had not found it.

In our culture, we have a tendency to think that when we finally have enough money to do anything we want, we'll be happy. But that's not where happiness is found. J. B. Phillips has said that our modern world has created its own beatitudes:

> Happy are the pushers, for they get on in the world.
> Happy are the hard-boiled, for they never let life hurt them.
> Happy are they who complain, for they get their own way in the end.
> Happy are the slave-drivers, for they get results.
> Happy are the knowledgeable, for they know their way around.
> Happy are the troublemakers, for they make people take notice of them.

The person who is poor in spirit is simply out of touch with the ways of the world. There is a tension between walking Christ's way and walking in the way of the world.

THOSE WHO ARE POOR IN SPIRIT WILL REALIZE THEIR EMPTINESS APART FROM GOD

The person who is poor in spirit doesn't boast of his talents or attainments because he knows he has nothing except from God. If he is gifted, it's because God gave him much. He is humble about his character, knowing he has nothing for which to be conceited. In his soul are the sins that put Christ on the cross. Those who are poor in spirit are the antithesis of the proud; they recognize their spiritual need. We are empty without God. We are impoverished without His blessing. We do not control our own destiny. If we build our dreams on the material world, at any moment they can be dashed.

When mighty Samson had his hair cut off, his strength was gone. Judges 16:20 tells us that Samson "did not know that the Lord had departed from him." He thought he could defeat the foe as he always had done, but now he was without the strength of the Lord. How sad is a man without power, and sadder still the man without power who doesn't know it. No man is so ignorant as he who knows nothing and knows not that he knows nothing! Perhaps you have had a chance to talk to someone like that recently. They try out their ignorance on you, and their utter lack of knowledge is sad. Samson thought he knew what he was doing, but he was utterly mistaken. He didn't know how poor he really was.

In Luke 12:16–21, the Lord Jesus told the story of a man with mistaken ideas of poverty and riches. In a self-centered soliloquy, the man says, "Soul, you have many goods laid up for many years; take your ease; eat, drink, and be merry." Then God said, "Fool! This night your soul will be required of you." Thinking his earthly riches made him righteous, the man was lost due to his own ignorance. "So is he who lays up treasure for himself, and is not rich toward God," added Jesus. If we lay up treasure in the outward kingdom, and never give attention to the inward kingdom, we'll never find happiness. Happiness is not an outward thing, but an inward thing. That's why Jesus said it's so hard for a rich man to get into heaven. He can't push away the things he owns and learn to depend upon the Lord.

The church at Laodicea was like that. Revelation chapter three tells us that the believers thought they were wealthy and in need of nothing, but God saw that they were actually poor, miserable, wretched, blind, and naked. The tragedy isn't that a person will be without what he needs. The tragedy is that a person will never recognize what he truly needs. No man can buy inner happiness. God alone grants happiness to those who seek Him. A person who doesn't understand that is to be pitied.

THOSE WHO ARE POOR IN SPIRIT WILL REACH OUT TO OTHERS WITH A SPIRIT OF LOVE AND COMPASSION

The world tells us to develop a thick skin. "Don't let others get close to you because if they're close, they can hurt you. Keep people away; emotion is a weakness." That's the spirit of this world. But if you read the New Testament, you'll find that the Spirit of the Lord says the exact opposite. Jesus wept at the tomb of His friend Lazarus. He took compassion on the lost crowds. He invested in close friendships with the disciples.

The kingdom of God is completely different from the kingdom of this world. A self-centered person won't notice anyone else; his concern is only for himself. He cannot be sensitive to those around him for fear their pain may ruin his happiness. But a person who is poor in spirit will look to minister. He will seek out those who are hurting so that he can heal the lives of others. A person filled up with himself is unable to reach out to others, for he loves only himself. A person who is poor in spirit will reach out to others in love.

Those Who Are Poor in Spirit Will Respond to Life with a Spirit of Gratitude

When the apostle Paul wrote to the Corinthians, he scolded them for being so proud of their spiritual gifts. They went around full of pride, talking about all the good qualities they had, but Paul's question was simple: "Who gave you those gifts?" God did. Why walk around acting proud as though your spiritual gifts were somehow earned when they were simply given by the grace of God? The poor-in-spirit person is humble, thanking God for all things because he recognizes that gifts are given by God out of grace and mercy, not because they are earned. Show me a man who is ungrateful, and I'll show you a man who isn't poor in spirit. Show me a woman who is unthankful, and I'll show you a woman who doesn't understand the first Beatitude.

Those Who Are Poor in Spirit Will Reach Their Highest Joy in Serving

Everybody wanted to lift Jesus up as king, but He simply said, "I did not come to be ministered unto, but to minister." A person who truly wants to be happy will find great joy in serving others. Phillip Yancey, a journalist who has had many opportunities to interview sports and entertainment stars, found that those with the highest profiles never seemed to be happy. They were nearly always unfulfilled, self-doubting, and unhappy. But those who had chosen to give their lives to service had a depth and richness that Yancey envied. The doctors working with outcasts, the missionaries translating the Bible into new languages, and the relief workers who had left high-paying jobs for obscurity and service were the ones who had found fulfillment and satisfaction in their lives. Some would argue that they were "wasting" their talents, but these people had discovered that true happiness is found not in getting what you want, but in giving to others what they need.

Don't search for happiness in the outward kingdom; you won't find it. Jesus said, "Blessed are the poor in spirit, for theirs is the kingdom of heaven." The person who is poor in spirit will experience a joy found only in heaven. He will understand what true happiness is—an inward happiness that God gives to those who call on Him.

APPLICATION

1. Read Matthew 23:1–39.

   a. What evidence of a lack of humility did Jesus identify in the Pharisees? (verses 5–7).

   b. What did Jesus say happens to those who exalt themselves? To those who humble themselves? (verse 12)

   c. The humble are already humble, and the prideful will be humbled, so everyone is going to end up humble (verse 12). Why is God so concerned about humility?

   d. Why were the Pharisees going to receive "greater condemnation?" (verses 13–14)

   e. What arrogant practice did Jesus condemn in verses 23–24?

f. What were the Pharisees like in spite of appearing righteous outwardly? (verse 28)

g. What would a truly humble religious leader never do? (verse 31)

h. How was the Pharisees' lack of humility ultimately demonstrated? (verse 37)

i. What is the connection between verses 38–39 and verse 12?

j. How does "poor in spirit" describe someone who is humble? What does "poor in spirit" mean?

k. If a humble person is poor in spirit, and the Pharisees were proud and arrogant, were they "rich in spirit?" Explain.

2. What did Jesus say about himself in Matthew 11:29?

3. What did Jesus mean by saying that the kingdom of heaven belongs to the poor in spirit? (Matthew 5:3)

   a. To what other character trait does Jesus assign the same benefit? (verse 10)

   b. What is it about humility and persecution that personifies the essence of the kingdom of heaven?

c. Can you think of any other character trait that personifies the kingdom of God?

d. Why do you think humility is not listed in Galatians 5:22–23?

e. What is the relationship between humility and the fruit of the Spirit?

f. Why do you think humility is not mentioned as an expression of love in 1 Corinthians 13:1–13?

g. What is the relationship between love and humility?

Happy Are the Humble • 31

4. Read Isaiah 14:13–14. List the five prideful statements made by the king of Tyre:

   a. I will . . .

   b. I will . . .

   c. I will . . .

   d. I will . . .

   e. I will . . .

   f. How is conceit related to pride? (1 Timothy 3:6)

DID YOU KNOW?

Matthew 5:1–12 is commonly referred to as the Beatitudes of Jesus. "Beatitudes" does not appear in our English Bibles; it is taken from the Latin *beatitudo* ("blessedness"), and was applied to this section of Matthew after it was compiled into the canon of the New Testament. Literary statements like the Beatitudes are also referred to as macarisms, from the Greek *makarios*, "blessed" or "happy," the word which usually introduces the statement of blessedness. Macarisms were found in Egyptian, Greek, and Hebrew literature, especially the Old Testament. Four of the Matthean beatitudes are also repeated in Luke 6:20–22.

LESSON 3

HAPPY ARE THE HURTING

Matthew 5:4

In this lesson we discover how God comforts those who mourn.

OUTLINE

The Bible is a book of paradoxes: We receive by giving, live by dying, and find by losing. Similarly, we can find true blessedness by mourning. Contrary to what our culture tells us, true happiness can be experienced when we mourn for ourselves and others.

I. Happiness Is Discovered When We Sacrifice the Present for the Future

II. Happiness Is Discovered When We Sympathize with Those Around Us Who Suffer

III. Happiness Is Discovered When We Sorrow for Our Own Sin

IV. Happiness Is Discovered When We Suffer the Losses and the Crosses of Life

OVERVIEW

"Blessed are those who mourn, for they shall be comforted." One of the most astounding truths about our generation is the belief that happiness and freedom from pain are our inalienable rights as American Christians. We believe that a man who manages his life well has the right to live above pain and enjoy happiness. And yet, deep down inside, we know that only children believe that pain always goes away. Pain is a part of life, and there is no guarantee of happiness.

Dr. Joseph Fabry has said that the focus of a man's life is the pursuit of meaning, not the pursuit of happiness. If we expect everything in life to be pleasurable, we invite frustration. In recent years, we have seen some preachers offer a "positive mental attitude" philosophy of life, negating the example in Scripture that hurt must sometimes happen. There has never been an attempt on the part of the biblical authors to give us a Pollyanna view of life. "Pack up your troubles in your old kit bag and smile, smile, smile" isn't found in the Old or New Testaments. Instead, the Bible offers a realistic appraisal of life in the human realm. Abraham cried when his wife Sarah died. David mourned over the loss of his son Absalom. Jeremiah, the "weeping prophet," preached his message of judgment with tears. A woman came to Jesus and washed His feet with her tears. The Lord himself wept at the death of His friend Lazarus. He anguished in the Garden of Gethsemane, watched Peter weep bitterly over his denial of Him, and comforted the weeping Mary Magdalene outside the tomb on Resurrection Morning. Where did we ever get the idea that there is something foreign about tears in life? Why do we think that tears are a sign of weakness or that they demonstrate a lack of faith in God? That's not the message of the Word of God.

There are all sorts of reasons for crying. There are tears of devotion, like Mary shed on Jesus' feet. There are tears of concern, like the apostle Paul cried as he preached to the Ephesians. There are tears of regret, like those shed by the Ephesian leaders as they said good-bye to Paul. There are tears of anguish, shed by the Lord as He wrestled over the will of God, and tears of compassion which Jesus wept as He gazed at the city of Jerusalem. And of course there are the tears of sorrow that accompany death and disappointment in this life. The Bible never asks us to pretend we don't hurt. It doesn't tell us to pretend sorrow is not real. You cannot make truth disappear merely by wishing it so. In fact, Psalm 56:8 says that

God bottles our tears and keeps them, so special are they to our heavenly Father. Yet, having said that, I struggle with Christ's teaching that those who mourn shall be happy. How can hurting and happiness be synonymous? What do tears have to do with laughter? There are at least four ways that happiness is discovered through hurting.

Happiness Is Discovered When We Sacrifice the Present for the Future

If a Christian accepts the crosses of life, he or she will ultimately be able to wear the crown. If we choose to live for the world to come, we may meet all kinds of sorrow, but we know that joy awaits us. In the story of Lazarus and Dives, the rich man cried out to Abraham in torment after his death. But he was told that he had received good things in this life, so he had punishment in the next life. That's the trade-off we face. We sacrifice present joy for future joy. We can take the easy road now and sacrifice the future, or we can sacrifice and discipline ourselves now so that we experience joy in the future. If we mourn now, we shall laugh later.

Students understand that truth. If they discipline themselves today, do their assignments, and keep up-to-date on their reading, they will do well at the end of the semester. Their sacrifice today will bring joy later. But if they decide to experience their joy now, putting parties ahead of homework, their joy now will result in mourning at the end of the semester when grades are posted. Jesus understood this principle. Happy are the hurting, for they shall be comforted. Happiness is discovered when we sacrifice the present for the future.

Happiness Is Discovered When We Sympathize with Those Around Us Who Suffer

Happiness belongs to those who feel sorrow for fellow men and women. Jesus was often described as a man full of compassion for others. He was constantly reaching out to heal and comfort those in pain. Sorrow is a product of love. As we love others, we hurt for their condition. As our love grows, it draws others into its circle. You can't mourn for someone you don't love. Imagine a man who never mourns. He lives by himself, having lost touch with his family and friends. He never visits anyone, nor is he visited. He is perfectly insulated against sorrow . . . but he is not happy. He has no one to share special moments with, no one with whom he can feel emotion.

The Bible says that when we suffer, we are able to help others who suffer. There is a blessing to those who can identify with pain, especially if they have experienced their own pain. Paul called God the "Father of mercies and God of all comfort, who comforts us in all our tribulation, that we may be able to comfort those who are in any trouble, with the comfort with which we ourselves are comforted by God" (2 Corinthians 1:3–4). In the midst of trouble, God offers a whole new inventory of tools to help those around you. How blessed to talk with somebody who has been through exactly what we're experiencing! Happy are those who can sympathize with the sorrowing people around them.

HAPPINESS IS DISCOVERED WHEN WE SORROW FOR OUR OWN SIN

In 2 Corinthians 7:10, we read, "For godly sorrow produces repentance leading to salvation, not to be regretted; but the sorrow of the world produces death." When was the last time you shed tears over the sin in your life? Generally in our culture, we simply don't deal with sin. The eminent psychologist Carl Menninger who studied the effects of sin in his famous book *Whatever Happened to Sin?* noted that when an individual fails to deal with the wrongs in his life, he never takes a step toward getting better. We call ourselves victims, always blaming someone else for our faults. A thief doesn't own up to his sin; he blames it on his deprived childhood. A murderer doesn't admit his sin; he blames it on abuse. But when a man faces up to the things in his life that he knows violate the holiness of God, he mourns over his own sin.

Have you ever come to God so brokenhearted over your failure that you wept? The Bible says that doing so is a cleansing step toward holiness and happiness in life. Blessed are they who mourn, for they shall be comforted. The man who cannot mourn over his own sin can never know the comfort and forgiveness of God. The Lord doesn't forgive sin we won't confess. But when we come to God, acknowledging what we have done and weeping in realization that it was our sin which helped nail Christ to the cross, God begins the healing process in our lives. Our hurt leads to the blessing of God's comfort.

As you study the life of Paul, you'll find that the older he got, the less impressed he became with himself. In his first letter, Galatians, he wrote, "Paul, an apostle . . . ." (Galatians 1:1). Seven years later, when he wrote his first letter to the Corinthians, he noted, "I am the least of the apostles, who am not worthy to be called an apostle" (1 Corinthians 15:9). Eight years after that, Paul said of himself, "To me, who am less than the least of all the saints . . ." (Ephesians 3:8). At this point Paul isn't talking about himself as an apostle, but as the least of all the saints. Late in his life, Paul wrote to his friend Timothy and said, "Christ Jesus came into the world to save sinners, of whom I am chief" (1 Timothy 1:15). In the span of a few years Paul went from being an apostle to being the chief sinner. The closer he got to the Lord, the more he realized the poverty of his own soul. Blessed are those who mourn over their own sin, shedding tears over the evil in their lives, for they can experience a wonderful peace in knowing that God cares and forgives them. They shall be comforted.

Happiness Is Discovered When We Suffer the Losses and the Crosses of Life

Sorrow has a value all its own. An old Arabian proverb says that "all sunshine makes a desert." You see, sorrow is the source for some of the greatest discoveries. The meaning of friendship and the meaning of love are often best found due to sorrow. It is in sorrow that a man discovers whether his faith is superficial or solid. In sorrow a man discovers God. The saddest thing in the world, according to James Reid, is not a soul that sorrows, but a heart so selfish and dull that nothing touches it. To sorrow is to love. "Mourning," according to Reid, "is indeed but another and deeper side of loving." The poet Robert Hamilton wrote, "I walked a mile with Pleasure, and she chattered all the way; but left me none the wiser for all she had to say. I walked a mile with Sorrow, and ne'er a word said she; but oh, the things I learned from her, when Sorrow walked with me!"

How do you deal with sorrow? Perhaps you've lost a loved one, or gone through a divorce, or lost your job. How does a Christian deal with grief? I've heard preachers give out some pretty bad counsel over the years. We've warned people to rest on the sovereignty of God, that what has happened is God's will, and that injustices will be made right in the next world. We are guilty of substituting fatalism for faith because many of life's disorders do not come from God. Some come from folly or sin. If I violate the principles of good health, God should not be blamed for my sickness and death. I've heard good people tell those in grief to resign themselves to sorrow, for that is the common lot of man. But the way the world deals with grief is far different from the way God tells us to deal with it.

First, God says to express grief, not repress it. Our culture says to bury the feelings. We don't want to be reminded of anything negative. But Jesus openly wept on at least three occasions. Expressing feeling is an emotional release, offering cleansing and freeing us to begin the journey toward hope.

Second, God says to face your loss, not replace it. Society's instruction is to get busy and fill your life with something else. Don't hang around a sad place. But that doesn't make it go away; it only buries the hurt like emotional toxic waste. The pattern in the Bible is to allow the full effect of sorrow to settle into our souls. There are no shortcuts to recovery. A person who reviews his loss, thinks it through, talks about it to friends and his Lord will begin to get through it.

Third, God says to reach out to others, not retreat from them. Our culture encourages us to leave grieving people alone, to "give them space." God's approach is the exact opposite. We are to grieve in community with one another. After Jesus' death, the disciples were all together, sharing their grief with one another. "Rejoice with those who rejoice," Paul tells us, "and weep with those who weep."

Fourth, God says to depend on the Comforter, not on the calendar. The normal counsel to one who is grieving is that "time heals all wounds." But the Bible says the Holy Spirit is the healer. The word Christ used to tell us that those who mourn shall be comforted is the very same word He used to explain the Holy Spirit. You may heal over time, but it is the Spirit doing the healing. The word is also translated "encouragement" or "made strong" because that's what the Spirit does when we mourn. In sadness, God is up to something. He wants to move you toward joy.

APPLICATION

1. Read James 4:4–10

   a. What was the general context that prompted these remarks from James? (see verses 1–3)

   b. What principle does James set forth as a backdrop for understanding discontent and strife? (verse 4)

   c. Who does God oppose, and who does He exalt? (verse 6)

   d. Who are we to resist, and who are we to draw near to? (verse 7)

   e. With what kind of attitude are we to draw near to God—pride or humility?

   f. What is the evidence of humility, at least concerning our sins? (verses 8–9)

g. What is God's ultimate goal for us? (verse 10b)

h. But what must happen first? (verse 10a)

i. What key word in John the Baptist and Jesus' preaching is the equivalent of "lament and mourn and weep?" (verse 9; see Matthew 3:2; 4:17)

j. Explain the connection between verses 1–4 and verses 8–10.

k. Describe the degree to which you experience mourning over your own sin and shortcomings in the spiritual life?

l. Spiritually, physically, emotionally—how do you "repent?"

2. Read Isaiah 61:1–3.

   a. What is the general theme of this passage?

   b. What was one of the purposes of the Messiah when He would come? (verse 2c–3)

   c. What would the Messiah give in exchange for their . . .
      - ashes (verse 3)

      - mourning (verse 3)

      - spirit of heaviness (verse 3)

   d. Who quoted parts of this passage in Luke 4:18–19?

Happy Are the Hurting • 41

e. How far did Jesus go before he stopped His quote from Isaiah?

f. Why do you think He did not quote the remainder of the passage (verses 2b–3)?

g. How is Matthew 11:28–30 a parallel to the Isaiah and Luke passages?

3. Read 2 Corinthians 1:3–7.

   a. How many different reasons can you think of for why a Christian might mourn?

   b. What name does Paul give to God in verse 3? Is God's comfort restricted to mourning for a particular reason or does He comfort all who mourn? (verse 4a)

c. What does God expect us to do with the comfort He provides for us? (verse 4b)

d. What kind of comfort has God provided for you in times of mourning?

e. How often are you able to use God's comfort to comfort others? Examples?

4. Read 2 Corinthians 7:8–12.

   a. What does Paul suggest is the goal of sorrow over sin? (verses 9–10)

   b. To what does the sorrow of the world lead? Why? (verse 10b)

Happy Are the Hurting • 43

c. What did the Corinthians' godly sorrow produce in them? (verse 11)

d. What did Paul prove to the Corinthians by chastising them for their tolerance of sin? (verse 12)

DID YOU KNOW?

Commentators point out that the first two of Jesus' beatitudes reflect the Old Testament theme of weeping and mourning over sin, only to find comfort in the restoration of joy and wholeness brought by the coming Messiah. When John the Baptist preached his inaugural sermons for the coming of Christ, his harsh-sounding tone was consistent with this theme: Joy in salvation comes only after broken-heartedness over sin. The hymn writer Charles Wesley captured this theme: "He speaks, and listening to his voice, new life the dead receive; the mournful, broken hearts rejoice, the humble poor believe." (*Expositor's Bible Commentary*, ref. Matthew 5:4)

LESSON 4

HAPPY ARE THE HARNESSED

Matthew 5:5

In this lesson we discover the true meaning of meekness.

OUTLINE

Look around today and you see people trying to increase their strength: working out at gyms, taking steroids to bulk up, and jockeying for position and power in business. Paradoxically, the Bible says true strength comes when we recognize our true weakness.

   I. The Meaning of Meekness in the Old Testament

  II. The Meaning of Meekness in the New Testament

 III. The Meaning of Meekness in Our Lives Today
   A. We Need Meekness to Receive God's Word
   B. We Need Meekness to Restore Fallen Christians
   C. We Need Meekness to Reach Others with the Gospel
   D. We Need Meekness to Remain Unified in Our Churches

OVERVIEW

Never are we more at odds with the world system than when we try to understand and live by the sayings of Jesus called the Beatitudes. We read them as His true words, but we wonder if anyone besides Jesus has ever lived their lives by them. Are they really practical? Do they really work?

If you thought that about the first two Beatitudes—happy are the humble and happy are the hurting—you'll think it even more about the third: Happy are the meek (Matthew 5:5). I think Don McCullough speaks for many of us when he writes about meekness:

> Meekness. Let's admit it. We don't like the word. It tastes insipid. It smells like morning mouth. It looks like Casper Milktoast. It has the strength of a cooked noodle. Coaches don't rally teams with meekness, executives don't send sales people into the field with it, and politicians don't promise to lead by it. Parents don't counsel their children on how to develop meekness. Generals don't embolden troops with a speech on meekness. You won't find anyone offering seminars on meekness training. It probably should be examined by the House Committee on Unamerican Activities. [McCullough, Donald W. *Finding Happiness in the Most Unlikely Places*. Downers Grove, IL: InterVarsity Press, n.d., p. 33.]

And the noted Bible commentator William Barclay echoes those sentiments with some of his own:

> To modern ears, the word meekness describes a weak, flabby, milk and water, spineless creature, lacking all virility, submissive and subservient to a fault, unable to stand up for himself or for anyone else, but that is very far from the original meaning of the word. The meaning of the word is so great and so comprehensive, that it almost defies translation. [Barclay, William. *The Beatitudes and the Lord's Prayer for Everyman*. New York: Harper & Row, Publishers, 1968, p. 38.]

Meekness may not seem like the American way, but it is definitely the biblical way to blessing from God. The Old Testament and New Testament differ slightly in their portrayal of meekness, and so we'll look at both to get the complete picture.

The Meaning of Meekness in the Old Testament

So much of what we read in the New Testament, especially in Jesus' words, has roots in the Old Testament. The beatitude about meekness is a good example, being taken by Jesus from the words of Psalm 37. There are at least five places in this psalm where the idea expressed in Jesus' beatitude is found, verse 11 being the closest:

- verse 9: ". . . those who wait on the Lord, they shall inherit the earth."
- verse 11: "But the meek shall inherit the earth . . . ."
- verse 22: "For those blessed by Him shall inherit the earth . . . ."
- verse 29: "The righteous shall inherit the land . . . ."
- verse 34: "Wait on the Lord, and keep His way, and He shall exalt you to inherit the land . . . ."

Two of the verses (9 and 34) speak about waiting on the Lord. That is perhaps the central idea behind meekness in the Old Testament. The meek person is the one who obediently accepts God's guidance, receives what God sends his way, and is compliant to the will of God. David, in Psalm 37, says this way of life leads to blessing, expressed in Old Testament terms as inheriting the land—the consummation of God's covenant promises to Israel.

Psalm 37 is a psalm I turn to in times of discouragement. David had times of discouragement in his life just like we do, and Psalm 37 is an expression of how he handled those times in his life. Look at David's advice for the discouraged:

- verses 1, 7, 8: "Do not fret . . . ." (Don't worry.)
- verse 3: "Trust in the Lord . . . ."
- verse 4: "Delight . . . in the Lord . . . ."
- verse 5: "Commit your way to the Lord . . . ."
- verse 7: "Rest in the Lord . . . ."

The way not to worry is to rest, trust, commit, and delight in the Lord. That is a definition of meekness. But meekness is not passivity, a kind of throwing in the towel. It is an active decision to wait . . . to rest . . . to trust . . . to leave matters in God's hands. Meekness is accepting God's will in your life with complete confidence that it is best.

Happy Are the Harnessed

We have examples in the Old Testament of people who were meek. Take Job, for instance. He went through more trouble than anybody, losing everything in his life except his wife (and even she criticized him mercilessly). His children, livestock, property—all were lost. And because he was a wealthy man to begin with, his losses were not incidental. Job wondered during all those trials why it was happening, yet was able to say, "The Lord gave, and the Lord has taken away; blessed be the name of the Lord" (Job 1:21). Even when the pressure got intense and he could find no answers for his suffering, he cried out, "Though He slay me, yet will I trust Him" (Job 13:15).

Sometimes the Lord lets us get to the end of ourselves in order for us to get to Him. And that's what happened to Job at the end of the book.

Another person in Scripture who lived a meek life was Mary, the Lord's mother. Think what it must have been like for a teenage girl in her culture to discover she was pregnant, being told by an angel that she had been chosen to be the mother of the Son of God. Mary's response to God epitomizes meekness: "Behold, the maidservant of the Lord! Let it be to me according to your word" (Luke 1:38). She could have protested, asked a thousand questions, or collapsed in fear at what her family and friends might say (not to mention Joseph, her intended husband). But she rested in the will of God for her life. She didn't fret—she trusted and committed and delighted in God. And that is meekness.

No doubt Jesus Himself is the greatest example of meekness in the Bible. In the Garden of Gethsemane, with the weight of the world's sin bearing down upon Him as He saw the cross of Calvary on the horizon, He said to His Father, "nevertheless not My will, but Yours, be done" (Luke 22:42). In the terms of Psalm 37, Jesus was saying, "I am waiting on the Lord, committing myself to Him. God is in control of my life. By trusting in Him, all will be well. By trusting in Him, I will inherit the blessings of His fulfilled promises for my life."

The Meaning of Meekness in the New Testament

When we get to the New Testament, we find that the meaning of meekness changes a bit. That's normal—words change in their usage and meaning over time, even biblical words.

Here's the basic idea: In the Old Testament, meekness meant to live under the control of God, to be God-controlled. In the New Testament, the circle tightens and the word refers more to self-control. Obviously, if a person is God-controlled, he is going to display characteristics of self-control. After all, being meek is one of the results of being under the control of the Holy Spirit ("gentleness" in the *NKJV*, Galatians 5:22–23).

Jesus defined himself as "gentle [meek] and lowly in heart" (Matthew 11:29); and in so doing, He personified a perfect definition of New Testament meekness: power under control. In the New Testament, a meek person can feel righteous indignation—righteous anger—in the right situations, as Jesus did. But a meek person never flies off the handle, out of control with his anger in a self-centered way. A meek person acts with power under control.

People often make Jesus out to be a caricature of a weakling: "gentle Jesus, meek and mild." Well, He was meek, but not in the negative sense we think of today. He was anything but that. "Weak" is certainly not the Jesus we read about in the four Gospels.

Once when Jesus healed a man with a withered hand, and the Pharisees criticized Him for healing on the Sabbath, Jesus "looked around at them with anger" because of the hardness of their hearts (Mark 3:5). Another time, when the disciples tried to keep little children from getting close to Jesus, He was "greatly displeased" (Mark 10:14). Yet another time, Jesus spoke bluntly about people who cause little children to stumble spiritually. It would be better, He said, for them to drown in the sea with a millstone around their neck! Not exactly a politically correct, tolerant way to put it.

Jesus' most famous display of power under control was when He entered the temple courts in Jerusalem to find them filled with merchants and money-changers. The priests in charge of the temple got greedy and began forcing people to buy sacrificial animals from them. They said the animals brought by worshipers had defects and weren't acceptable, and they forced the people to buy animals from them at inflated prices. It was extortion! When Jesus entered the courts and saw what was going on, He began turning the tables of the merchants over and driving them and the money-changers from the temple precinct with a whip made from cords. "Gentle Jesus, meek and mild" didn't look weak that day. He displayed His righteous indignation at what the priests had done to His Father's house of worship.

Happy Are the Harnessed

Meekness never gets angry at what happens to itself. It only gets angry at what happens to others. Jesus never reacted in anger when He was personally abused at His trial and crucifixion: "He did not threaten, but committed himself to Him who judges righteously" (1 Peter 2:23). But unrighteousness in the temple, or abuse of others . . . these things aroused His righteous anger. Jesus was meek, not weak.

I love what Thomas Brown said: "Meekness is taking injuries like we take pills—not chewing them, but swallowing them whole." [*Webster's New World Dictionary of Quotable Definitions*. Ed. Eugene R. Brussell. Englewood Cliffs, NJ, 1988, p. 360.] His meaning is that we are not to dwell on them, but to deal with them quickly—then let them go. Anyone who has ever been injured by another has had to practice letting go of anger—committing the offense to "Him who judges righteously."

The Meaning of Meekness in Our Lives Today

There are four areas where meekness is a critical quality, places where power under control will determine our ability to be effective.

We Need Meekness to Receive God's Word

James 1:21 says we need meekness to receive God's Word: "Receive with meekness the implanted word." Many people in our culture don't know they need to receive God's Word. It is available to them, but they assume they don't need it. They believe their own wisdom is sufficient to get them through life. But it's impossible to be filled with man's wisdom and God's wisdom at the same time. Nobody who is not meek says, "Lord, I yield up my own understanding to You. I submit my life to Your direction as contained in Your Word." Only by submitting ourselves to the Spirit of God will the Word of God make sense to our human minds. And the power to submit in that way is the power of meekness, the power to recognize that God's Word and wisdom are better than our own.

We Need Meekness to Restore Fallen Christians

Galatians 6:1 tells us we need meekness to restore a fallen brother or sister in Christ. Great power under control is needed to minister to a fallen Christian soldier—the power not to be judgmental and the power not to fall into the same failure ourselves. Someone has said that meekness is the spirit that makes correction a stimulant instead of a depressant. That means you can lift a person up out of despair and give them hope for the future. Far too often we act toward those who have sinned as though we have never fallen ourselves. We talk about them on the prayer chain under the guise of asking for prayer. And even if they are restored to fellowship we find it hard to treat them as a forgiven and repentant person. That is not meekness. Meekness acknowledges that there, but for the grace of God, might go I.

We Need Meekness to Reach Others with the Gospel

First Peter 3:15 says, "Always be ready to give a defense to everyone who asks you a reason for the hope that is in you, with meekness and fear." We would win more people to Christ if we witnessed to them with meekness.

When I was a young pastor in Indiana, our church had an evangelism program that involved door-to-door visitation. One day I received a phone call from a businessman in town who had been visited the night before by a member of our church. He was not happy with how the meeting had gone. He said the man who visited him would not leave unless he prayed a prayer with him. "So I prayed the doggone prayer," he said, just so the man would leave. He told me his only prayer now was that he would not receive any more such visitors from our church. And he hung up.

I'm sure our church member meant well, but he did more harm than good in that particular visit. Meekness will do far more to represent Christ faithfully than will overbearing and aggressive witnessing.

We Need Meekness to Remain Unified in Our Churches

If we take Paul's words in Ephesians 4:2–3 to heart, we will preserve the unity in our churches "with all lowliness and gentleness [meekness], with longsuffering, bearing with one another in love, endeavoring to keep the unity of the Spirit in the bond of peace."

Maintaining unity in church requires "endeavoring." That is, it requires work. Sinful people do not naturally strive to submit to one another and yield to one another. Such unity only happens supernaturally—that is, with meekness. In any gathering of people, there will be pockets of power that develop. If unity is to be maintained, it will be because people willingly direct their power toward the goal of unity. And that will only happen if they are people of meekness—people whose power is under control. Lowliness and gentleness allow people to yield to a greater good than their own self-interests. In churches that have split over divisive issues, you can be assured that meekness is missing.

Jesus said the meek will inherit the earth, which in the Old Testament referred to the promised land of Canaan. In the New Testament, it refers to the blessings of all the promises of God—which include a new heaven and new earth. The meek are not weak. They are happy (blessed) now and will be happy for eternity.

APPLICATION

1. The beatitude Jesus spoke concerning meekness is taken from Psalm 37:11. Answer the following questions from Psalm 37.

   a. What is the general subject of this psalm? (verses 1–3)

   b. Instead of fearing the wicked, what are we to do? (verse 3)

   c. What characterizes the person described in verses 4–5?

   d. What does it mean to "delight yourself also in the Lord?" (verse 4a)

   e. What aspect of meekness is found in verses 7–8?

   f. Instead of not resting, not waiting, and do not fret, what would a person without meekness do when attacked by evildoers?

   g. How do words like rest, wait, and do not fret help you understand the meaning of meekness?

   h. Using those words as guides, how meek are you? What do you tend to do when life goes against you in some way?

Happy Are the Harnessed

i. What happens when we fail to manifest meekness? (verse 8)

j. Compare verse 9 with verse 11. Since both verses mention inheriting the earth, how would you define a meek person?

k. For an Old Testament saint, what did "inherit the earth" refer to? (verse 29)

l. When Jesus repeats this promise in the New Testament (to Jews and Gentiles) to what does it refer? (Consider Revelation 21:1)

m. What is the difference between the meek and the arrogant? (verse 22)

n. Why does it pay to remain meek in the face of danger? (verses 25, 28)

o. Based on the promises in this psalm, what is another synonym for "meek?" (verse 39)

p. With what summary promise does David conclude this psalm about the meek—the one who waits upon the Lord? (verse 40)

2. Waiting on the Lord is characteristic of the meek. What do you find in the following verses about those who wait on the Lord?

   a. Isaiah 30:18

   b. Isaiah 40:31

   c. Lamentations 3:25

   d. Psalm 27:14

   e. When do you find it hardest to wait upon the Lord?

   f. Give an example of a time when waiting on the Lord, instead of rushing ahead with your agenda, proved to be the right thing to do.

3. Who is God going to watch out for when it comes to judgment? (Isaiah 11:4)

   a. What is the relationship between meekness and justice? (Zephaniah 2:3)

b. With what is meekness made synonymous in Zephaniah 3:12?

c. What similarity do you find between the "meekness and gentleness of Christ" and the need to "speak the truth in love?" (2 Corinthians 10:1; Ephesians 4:15)

4. Explain Christ's actions in Matthew 21:12 with being a meek person.

DID YOU KNOW?

The basic meaning of the Greek word behind "meek" (*praus*) is "gentle," from which is derived *prautes*, "gentleness" or "meekness." But the Greek scholar W. E. Vine warns against misunderstanding the meaning of this latter word: "It must be clearly understood, therefore, that the meekness manifested by the Lord and commended to the believer is the fruit of power. The common assumption is that when a man is meek, it is because he cannot help himself; but the Lord was 'meek' because He had the infinite resources of God at His command. Described negatively, meekness is the opposite to self-assertiveness and self-interest; it is equanimity of spirit that is neither elated nor cast down, simply because it is not occupied with self at all." (*Vine's Complete Expository Dictionary*, p. 401.)

LESSON 5

HAPPY ARE THE HUNGRY

Matthew 5:6

In this lesson we discover what it means to be hungry for God—and how to be filled.

OUTLINE

Cable TV shows on cooking, magazines devoted to food, diet plans—food is a consuming topic in our culture. Many people mistake physical hunger for spiritual hunger and remain unfilled. Only God can satisfy the deepest hunger of the soul.

I. **Spiritual Hunger Is the Reality of Your Faith**

II. **Spiritual Hunger Is the Requirement for Your Growth**

III. **Lack of Spiritual Hunger Is the Reason for Your Spiritual Failure**
   A. How Do I Know if I'm Hungry for God?
   B. What Do I Do if I Don't Have Hunger for God?

OVERVIEW

Blessed are those who hunger and thirst for righteousness, for they shall be filled" (Matthew 5:6). Hunger is something you come across every day. There are young businessmen whom we describe as "hungry" because they want to make the sale so badly that they'll do nearly anything. There are athletes whom we describe as "hungry" because they go all out to win. And there are people who so want to know God better that they can be described as "spiritually hungry." A. W. Tozer once noted that the great people of Christendom have had an insatiable hunger for God. The esteemed missionary Hudson Taylor wrote, "I saw Him, and I sought Him, and I had Him, and I wanted Him." He was hungry for God. That's a characteristic of those who walk with God and experience the joy of knowing Him.

In Psalm 27:4, David describes his relationship with God by saying, "One thing I have desired of the LORD, that will I seek: That I may dwell in the house of the LORD all the days of my life, to behold the beauty of the LORD, and to inquire in His temple." The desire to know God was at the center of David's life. The sons of Korah reveal a similar theme in Psalm 42:1: "As the deer pants for the water brooks, so pants my soul for You, O God." And Psalm 63:1–2 reads, "O God, You are my God; early will I seek You; my soul thirsts for You; my flesh longs for You in a dry and thirsty land where there is no water. So I have looked for You in the sanctuary, to see Your power and Your glory."

The psalmists had a deep hunger for God. Throughout Psalm 119 you can find illustrations of that desire. In verse 34 the author says he wants God's word in his heart. Verse 40 speaks of longing after God's truth, and verse 58 entreats God's favor with the psalmist's whole heart. "I cry out with my whole heart," we read in verse 145. All of those verses reveal a longing to know God. If you've ever worked with someone who approached the job in a half-hearted way, you know how frustrating it can be. But the psalmist was whole-hearted when it came to knowing God. To give everything toward seeking Him—that is the essence of spiritual hunger. All of the great men and women of God have had it. Moses, Elijah, Isaiah, David, and John had a hunger for God. Luther, St. Francis, Pliny, and Thomas à Kempis thirsted after the Lord. They sought the Lord and weren't satisfied by anything other than a close walk with Him.

You know, I am convinced that we have as much of God as we really want. You may claim to want more of God in your life, but you already have as much as you want. If you've ever been thirsty on a hot day, you know what it is to long for water. Most of us don't long for God with that sort of passion. We want a convenient religion—one that can fit into our schedules without too much difficulty. We want God in our lives, but we don't want to be fanatics. Yet Jesus said that it is the spiritually hungry and thirsty who will be happy, for they'll be filled with the satisfying presence of the Lord.

SPIRITUAL HUNGER IS THE REALITY OF YOUR FAITH

This verse may be the most demanding of the Beatitudes. Jesus wants His people to hunger and thirst after God. Yet it also shows how Jesus views our struggles. He did not say, "Blessed are they who attain righteousness," or none of us could be blessed. Christ didn't permit happiness only to the spiritually mature, but to all who desire and seek after maturity. If you have a desire within you to know God better, to understand His Word better, and to live this life more authentically for the Lord, the very wanting of it is evidence that you already belong to God. In our world today, many people call themselves Christians, but they don't seek after the things of God. They don't have any desire for the things of God. They have an entry-level relationship with the Almighty, so they assume they are on their way to heaven and need nothing more. But if there isn't a holy dissatisfaction in your heart about your spiritual life, and a hungering and thirsting to go farther with God, then there is something missing in your faith. I love God, but the Bible tells me that I am to grow in my ability to love God. I love God's Word, but the Bible says that I am to be growing in my hunger for it. Spiritual hunger is a blessed evidence within our hearts that we truly belong to Him. If you are unhappy with your spiritual life, that's a good sign. So am I. I want to know God better. That's simply the reality of being a Christian.

SPIRITUAL HUNGER IS THE REQUIREMENT FOR YOUR GROWTH

A rich young ruler once came to Jesus in search of eternal life. Jesus was impressed with the man, for he was attractive, successful, and seeking the right things. The Bible tells us that Jesus loved him. So the Lord told him to sell everything he had and give the money away. I don't believe that simply having money was the problem. The issue was one of spiritual hunger. In essence, Jesus was saying,

"If you don't want Me more than you want money, you're not going to make it." Christ wants us to have a hunger for himself.

Early in His ministry, Jesus was being followed by great crowds of people. They wanted the miracles and the ministry of Jesus, but not the commitment He demanded. One day the Lord simply stood up and said, "Let Me tell you what it's going to take if you want to follow Me. You will have to deny yourself. You will have to leave home and family. There will be divisions in relationships. You may be called by God to suffer hurts, injustice, and pain. But unless you are willing to do those things and make Me first, you are not worthy to be My disciples." Suddenly there were no longer any crowds following Jesus. The thing that separates people from the Lord is the thing we call spiritual hunger—the desire to know God above all else. If you want to grow in Christ, you must have spiritual hunger.

THE LACK OF SPIRITUAL HUNGER IS THE REASON FOR YOUR SPIRITUAL FAILURE

Sometimes we don't sufficiently want to be Christians. We claim that we do, but we aren't willing to do the hard things necessary. I've seen businessmen and athletes achieve success by sheer force of their desires, but I know few Christians willing to sacrifice anything to find God. Dan Henning, a former head coach in the National Football League, once told me that what separates a great quarterback from a good quarterback is the intangibles. The great ones have an inner toughness and desire to succeed. They hunger to win football games.

One of the secrets to success and achievement is desire. To be a mighty man or woman of God requires first a great desire in your heart to know God. If you're happy just to be in the game, you won't accomplish much for Him. The secret to making a difference for God in this world is desire. The apostle Paul was a man of desire. He had some great experiences, including three visions of Jesus which included things he couldn't even describe. At the end of his life, Paul said that the desire of his life was to know Christ. He hadn't yet arrived, but was pressing ahead toward God. The closer he got to his goal, the more he gave himself to it. It's easy to be a mediocre Christian with nice friends, celebratory worship, and interesting classes about the faith. But if we allow the perks of the church to run our lives, we will always remain on an immature level with God. And the truth is, we'll never really be happy. There is no challenge, no excitement, and no adventure in mediocrity. If you really want to know God, if you really want to be happy, you'll develop a hunger and thirst for Him.

How Do I Know if I'm Hungry for God?

So consider two insightful questions for your spiritual life. First, are you satisfied with yourself? The Puritans used to say, "He has the most need of righteousness who least wants it." If you are smug and self-satisfied, you aren't hungry; and God wants you hungry. A person hungering and thirsting after righteousness has a desire for God's Word. It's funny how that spiritual hunger works, for it's the exact opposite of physical hunger. With physical hunger, you get hungry when you don't eat. Once you've eaten, you are no longer hungry. With spiritual hunger, the more you eat, the hungrier you get. When you stop partaking of spiritual food through the Word of God, you lose your appetite. The more you get into the Bible, the more you begin to make sense of God's Word in your life and the greater your appetite. I've got friends who are memorizing the book of Romans, and their spiritual appetite has increased dramatically since they began.

Perhaps there was a time in your life when you were really hungry for God's Word. If you're not now, it's time you began reading your Bible again. As you begin to partake of the Word, your appetite for it will return. If you've gone through the process of pushing God out of your life, force-feed yourself. Sit down, open up your Bible, and start to read. If you start to fall asleep, read it aloud. Keep reading, and eventually God will speak to your heart. There will be a new fire in your soul. You'll experience a new love for God. The more you do it, the more you'll want to do it. If you are struggling with the language, get yourself a modern translation of the Scriptures. If you don't spend time reading your Bible, you'll never develop a hunger and thirst for God. And without a hunger and thirst for righteousness, you cannot be filled. Your life will be one of unfulfillment, never filled up with the Lord.

What Do I Do if I Don't Have Hunger for God?

There is a second question that you need to consider, one that you must answer in the quietness of your own heart. As you examine your relationship with the Lord, are you hungry for God? Do you have as much of Him as you really want? Are you satisfied with where you are with God? Or do you want more? Those who hunger and thirst after righteousness will one day be filled. If you want to have that satisfaction of being filled up with God, develop your hunger for Him now.

APPLICATION

1. Read Isaiah 55:1–2. (The context of this passage is that exiled Israel is being invited to return from spiritual and physical barrenness in Babylon.)

   a. What does the word "thirst" imply about their spiritual condition? (verse 1)

   b. What do "the waters" represent? How did Jesus use this theme? (John 7:37–38)

   c. To what did Jesus refer specifically in talking about "living water?" (John 7:39)

   d. What would have been the exiles' economic condition after having been in captivity? (Isaiah 55:1)

   e. How did Isaiah use these economic terms to picture their spiritual resources? (verse 1)

   f. Even if they had money, what good would it do in terms of acquiring spiritual food?

g. How does Isaiah compare the satisfaction levels of physical food verses spiritual food? (verse 2)

h. How could spiritual food be offered to Israel for free? Who paid for it? (Isaiah 53:5–9)

i. What were milk and honey symbols of in agrarian and economic terms? (Exodus 3:8)

j. What had Israel been used to in captivity? (Ezekiel 19:13)

k. What is the spiritual significance of what God is offering Israel? (In spite of their sin, they were being offered "the best" God had to offer.) How does this compare with the gospel of Jesus Christ? (Romans 5:8; Ephesians 1:7)

l. What exhortation does Isaiah offer in 55:6? Is a day coming when the free spiritual food and drink will no longer be available?

m. What does God promise to those who come to Him? (verse 7)

Happy Are the Hungry • 63

2. How would you describe your own spiritual and emotional "filling" since becoming a Christian? How near empty were you, and how has that changed?

3. Read Psalm 63:1–11.

   a. Where was David when he wrote this psalm (see the superscription of the psalm in the title)?

   b. What was he doing there? (verse 9)

   c. With what confession does David begin this psalm of praise?

   d. How would one naturally feel in such a situation (pursued by enemies, hiding in the wilderness)—empty or filled?

   e. What was David's spiritual condition in spite of his circumstances? (verses 4–5)

f. How did David remain filled with the presence of God?

- Where? (verses 2, 7)

- How? (verse 4)

- When? (verses 1, 6)

g. What did David value more than his physical life? (verse 3)

h. What was David's spiritual condition as a result of his efforts? (verse 5a)

4. Read Psalm 42:1–11.

   a. What are David's circumstances? (verses 5, 9–10)

   b. What was his strategy for staying alive spiritually? (verses 1–2a)

   c. What measure of confidence did he have in God's answering him? (verse 8)

   d. What counsel did David give himself? (verse 11)

   e. What counsel would David give you in times of spiritual emptiness?

DID YOU KNOW?

The word for "filled" in Matthew 5:6 is primarily a gastronomical term—it refers to people or animals being filled with food (*chortazo*). When used in a spiritual sense, the reference to physical eating provides a well-known reference. It is used in Matthew 14:20 to refer to the 5,000 who were fed by Jesus and were so "filled" that there were twelve baskets of leftovers. In Revelation 19:21, birds come and "fill" themselves ("gorged themselves," *NIV*; "held a feast," *The Message*) on the flesh of the enemies of God following Armageddon. The apostle Paul uses the word to describe the opposite of being hungry (Philippians 1:11).

LESSON 6

HAPPY ARE THE HELPERS

Matthew 5:7

*In this lesson we explore the meaning of mercy—
how to extend it and what happens when we do.*

OUTLINE

Somewhere along the way—probably when you were a child or adolescent—you were spared the negative results of an act for which you deserved punishment. When that happened, you received mercy: being spared a negative consequence you deserved.

I. What Is Mercy?

II. How Is Mercy Expressed?

III. What Are the Results of Mercy?

OVERVIEW

"Blessed are the merciful, for they shall obtain mercy" (Matthew 5:7). Some years ago Lorraine Hansberry wrote a successful play entitled *A Raisin in the Sun*. In the play, an African-American family inherits ten thousand dollars from a life insurance policy, and the mother sees that money as a chance to help her family escape from the ghetto and move into a real house in the country. Her daughter, a brilliant student, wants to use the money to fulfill her dream of going to medical school. But her son convinces everyone that he can take the money, start a business with a friend, and accomplish all those things. He promises the family that if they will give him the money, he'll return all the blessings their hard lives have denied them.

Against her better judgment, the mother gives her son the money, believing that he deserves a chance to succeed. But the son's "friend" skips town with the money, and the young man must face his family and admit that all their hopes for the future have been dashed. His sister lashes out at him with a barrage of ugly epithets. She calls him every despicable thing you can imagine. Her contempt has no limits, and when her mother interrupts by saying, "I thought I taught you to love your brother," the girl replies, "Love him? There's nothing left to love!"

Then, in a way that shows she understands mercy, the mother responds,

> There is always something left to love. If you ain't learned that, you ain't learned nothin'. Have you cried for that boy today? I don't mean for yourself and the family because we lost all that money. I mean for him, for what he's been through, and what it's done to him. Child, when do you think it's the time to love somebody the most? When they done good and made things easy for everybody? Well then, you ain't through learnin' because that ain't the time at all. It's when he's at his lowest and can't believe in himself 'cause the world done whipped him so. When you starts measurin' somebody, measure him right, child. Measure him right. Make sure you done taken into account what hills and valleys he come through before he got to wherever he is. That's mercy. And child, you need to learn mercy.

What Is Mercy?

Mercy is love that is given when it is not deserved. It is forgiveness that is given when it is not earned. It is a gift that flows like a refreshing stream to quench the fires of angry, condemning words. It is called mercy; and in our day, it's almost a forgotten quality.

Some time ago, *Christianity Today* reported that seminary students were upset about something a reporter had learned. It seems a couple of researchers decided to find out if those preparing for the ministry were also Good Samaritans. They met individually with forty seminary students and taped interviews with them as they walked along a particular path. They were asked questions about their careers and concerns for the future; then they were asked to talk about the parable of the Good Samaritan. On cue, a hired actor dressed as a bum would groan and slump to the ground in front of them. More than half the students walked right on by. Some literally stepped over the slumped body as they hurried to tell their story.

Those seminarians are probably no different from most of us. We live in a world with a closed heart, closed hand, and closed home. Many of us have shut ourselves up because of the risk of involvement. The hard, isolated, and uncompassionate characteristic of society has crept into our lives so that we don't want to worry about anybody else. "Think about Number One," the world says to us. "Don't open your eyes to the needs of people. Look after yourself first."

But the Bible suggests a different standard. The Greek word for "mercy" literally means "full of pity." It describes someone with a sympathetic heart and is often used to describe the Lord Jesus. In Matthew chapter 15, we read of the compassion Christ had for a demon-possessed woman. In chapter 18, Jesus shows compassion for a man in debt; and in chapter 20, He has compassion on two blind men. In Mark 5, we read about Christ's compassion for a man in need of deliverance. For Christians, mercy is a Spirit-guided ability to manifest practical, compassionate, and cheerful love toward someone who is suffering. In the New Testament, it most often refers to those who might be easily ignored—the crippled, the sick, the deformed, the aged, or the mentally ill. Those less fortunate than ourselves are the ones to whom we ought to show mercy. Mercy is one of the noblest virtues. It dares to express tenderness in the midst of a harsh and cruel world. Our world preaches that you'll be happiest when you forget about others and focus on yourself, but Jesus said that those who exhibit mercy will be happy.

How Is Mercy Expressed?

In Luke chapter ten, Jesus told a story of a Samaritan who was willing to step out of the context of his day and act differently than the lawyers and priests of the first century. The Lord said that a man fell among thieves, was beaten, bruised, and left for dead. It's clear that religion wasn't the solution he needed, for all the religious people passed by: a priest, a Levite, and a lawyer who spent his time studying the Law of God. But a Samaritan, who was hated by the Jews, became the hero of Jesus' story. He stopped to minister to this unfortunate one, to a man he didn't know. Luke 10 says that he had compassion on him. The Samaritan's heart was moved by what he saw. He took that bleeding man and bound up his wounds, used an antiseptic, and poured oil on him to soothe the pain. Rather than just saying a prayer for him, the Samaritan exhibited real love by taking care of someone else in need.

A careful reading of the story reveals that it cost the Samaritan to minister. The act of mercy on his part wasn't without cost. There was no "easy grace." He took out of that which was his own to help another. He paid for the oil and the medicine. He gave the wounded man transportation. He gave up time in his schedule to care for this stranger and even paid for the man to stay at an inn until he was better. You can't show mercy without having it cost you something. And all this was done by a despised Samaritan, who wouldn't even have been greeted by a passing Jew. Christ noted that to put pressure on the religious people of His day. In essence, Jesus was saying, "Even the hated Samaritan knows how to show mercy. Why don't you?"

At the end of the story, Jesus asked, "Which of these three do you think was neighbor to him who fell among the thieves—the priest, the Levite, or the Good Samaritan?" The lawyer answered, "He who showed mercy on him." Mercy is the quality of the Good Samaritan, and Jesus instructs us to "Go and do likewise." Mercy is what the Samaritan did when he reached out to someone who could not pay him back, who was hurting and in need. We need to learn to express that virtue in the church. It's easy to want to travel in circles where everything is beautiful and everyone is like us. But the Bible says that we'll find happiness when we learn to show mercy to those who aren't quite as nicely dressed or as educated and refined as we are.

I read an article recently about a young Christian nurse who decided she was going to manifest mercy. One of her patients was a woman in a vegetative state. She'd had a cerebral aneurism and was completely brain dead, unaware of anything around her. To make it easier to care for her, the staff became emotionally detached. The patient was treated like a "thing," not a person, by the hospital staff. But this young nurse couldn't treat anyone like that. She talked to the patient, offering friendliness and encouragement, even though she knew the patient couldn't reciprocate. When the nurse was scheduled to work on a holiday, she made it a point to be extra positive. As she was taking care of things in the room, she suddenly noticed the patient was looking at her, crying. It was the only emotion she had ever shown, and it changed the attitude of the entire staff toward her. The nurse later said that she owed that patient quite a lot. Without that experience, she might never have known what it was like to give herself completely to someone who could offer nothing in return. That's the true spirit of mercy.

What Are the Results of Mercy?

Jesus said that the merciful would obtain mercy. If you show mercy to someone else, you get mercy back. We have received mercy from God, so we ourselves can show mercy to others. As we understand the depth of God's mercy, we are compelled to be merciful toward others.

Jesus once said, "For with what judgment you judge, you will be judged; and with the measure you use, it will be measured back to you" (Matthew 7:2). If you forgive others, God will also forgive you. But if you are unforgiving, you will find the Lord that same way. "For judgment is without mercy to the one who has shown no mercy," it says in James 2:13. As a man judges, so will he be judged. If mercy is the characteristic of God, then someone who practices it will become more and more like God every day. But he who makes no attempt to show mercy distances himself from God and demonstrates that he does not know Him.

Peter once asked Jesus how many times he should forgive someone. Thinking himself generous, Peter suggested the number seven. But the Lord laughed off that number and suggested it was more like seventy times seven. Then Jesus told the story of a man who owed a king a great sum of money but was unable to pay it back. He was mercifully forgiven the debt, but that same man then went out and had another man arrested for not paying him back ten dollars! The king was furious when he found out about it and had the ungrateful wretch arrested until he could pay back every penny. And the Lord finished His story by saying, "So my heavenly Father also will do to you if each of you, from his heart, does not forgive his brother his trespasses" (Matthew 18:35). What made it mandatory that the ten dollar debt be forgiven? The fact that his own huge debt had been cancelled.

We have been forgiven a great debt by our heavenly Father, one we could never repay. Our sin debt was so great that no amount of good works or sacrifice could ever take care of it. "The wages of sin is death," we are told in Romans 6:23. But when Christ died on the cross, He forgave us freely of everything we have ever done. He has shown us great mercy. So what should we do when confronted by someone who needs our mercy? We are to extend mercy. It's our responsibility, by the grace of God, to show mercy to those around us. It doesn't always happen in the church because we want people to live up to our expectations and "earn" our love, but that's not the system Christ put into place. He wants us to love others, even when they don't deserve it. We are all flawed human beings in need of mercy.

In Morton Thompson's novel, *Not as a Stranger*, a young doctor accuses an older physician of malpractice. Brilliant and capable, but impatient and intolerant, the young doctor sits before a review committee to discuss the charges. The men on the committee are older and ask the young man not to act hastily, but to consider the actions of the older doctor as a difference of opinion. Any man in the zealousness of youth tends to judge others more harshly. But that young doctor will not retract his accusation. So the president of the medical association leans across his desk, looks the young man right in the eyes, and says, "If you persist in bringing formal charges, then be sure of one thing: Don't ever, ever, as long as you live, make a mistake." The way we treat others is the way we'll be treated. And the good news is that if you will show mercy to others, even when they don't deserve it, the result will be happiness.

Ask God to give you sensitivity to those around you. Look for people with needs, and then reach out in mercy and meet them. The world says to look out for yourself, but the Lord says to look out for others. The world wants you to believe that you'll be happy when you take care of yourself, but nobody is really happy in a selfish world—they're alone. Happiness is found in ministering to others. The merciful will obtain mercy and will find true happiness in being merciful to others.

APPLICATION

1. Read Matthew 20:29–34.

    a. What did the two men ask Jesus for? (verses 30–31)

    b. What was Jesus' response to the men? (verse 34)

    c. When the blind men asked for _____, Jesus responded by having _____ on them.

    d. In a similar situation in Luke 17:11–19, what did the lepers ask Jesus for? (verse 13)

    e. And in Matthew 9:27–31? (verse 27)

Happy Are the Helpers • 73

f. Why is "mercy" the right word in these situations? (Why didn't the men ask for "kindness" or "love" or "healing?" Why did they cry out for mercy?)

g. How would you define mercy?

h. What aspect of mercy is revealed in these situations: the withholding of consequences due, or the bestowing of help needed?

2. Read Luke 15:11–32.

   a. What did the younger son do that was foolish—that you could guess would not end well for him? (verses 11–12)

   b. What did he eventually do? (verses 13)

c. What did he do to stay alive? (verses 14–16)

d. From a cause-and-effect perspective, would you say he deserved the life he ended up with? Why?

e. When he returned home, what emotion did his father feel when he saw his foolish son? (verse 20)

f. What did the father do that was merciful? (verses 22–24)

g. What might his father have been justified in doing, instead of what he did?

Happy Are the Helpers • 75

h. The father did not give his son what he _____,
   but gave him what he didn't _____ instead.

i. How would you assess the older brother's measure of mercy toward his younger brother? (verses 28–30)

j. Someone always pays so that mercy can be extended. Who paid in the case of the prodigal son?

k. Who paid in our situation as lost and prodigal sinners? (Mark 10:45)

l. What did we not get that we deserved? What did we get that we didn't deserve?

76 • *How to Be Happy According to Jesus*

3. Why do you think Paul called God "the Father of mercies?" (2 Corinthians 1:3) (Think: If the Wright brothers were the "fathers of modern flight," what does that mean? What is the parallel with "Father of mercies?")

4. Read Matthew 18:23–35.
   a. What did the man in debt receive from his creditor? (verse 27)

   b. What was the basis of the creditor's actions? (verse 27)

   c. What degree of mercy and compassion did the debtor exercise in his own role as creditor? (verse 30)

   d. What did the original debtor receive that he actually deserved? (verse 34)

Happy Are the Helpers • 77

e. What is Jesus' warning for those who, from their heart, do not forgive others of their trespasses? (verse 35)

f. In light of the forgiveness we have received from God, what ought we to do for others? (Ephesians 4:32)

DID YOU KNOW?

One of the primary root words for mercy in the Old Testament is *r-h-m* (*raham*, to be merciful; *rehem*, mercy). *Rehem* is also the word for "bowels" or "womb," and its use for compassion or mercy signified the deepest-seated human emotions, feelings emanating from the center of one's being. For instance, 1 Kings 3:26 literally says, "her bowels yearned upon her son," (KJV) but is translated in English as "she yearned with compassion for her son." (See also Genesis 43:30 where Joseph had compassion on his younger brother Benjamin.) Given the root meaning of *rehem*, there is no deeper human feeling in the Old Testament language than mercy and compassion.

LESSON 7

Happy Are the Holy

Matthew 5:8

In this lesson we define "pure heart" and learn how to develop purity.

OUTLINE

During flu season we are reminded of strategies for remaining healthy: Stay out of crowded places, wash your hands often, don't eat or drink after others. To stay spiritually healthy, we need a wellness strategy: a way to keep our hearts clean and undefiled by sin.

I. Purity of the Heart

II. Purity Portrayed
   A. Perfect Purity
   B. Positional Purity
   C. Practical Purity

III. The Path to Purity
   A. Covenant with Your Eyes
   B. Consecrate Your Mind
   C. Commit to Bible Memorization
   D. Counteract Satan's Strategy

Happy Are the Holy • 79

OVERVIEW

"Blessed are the pure in heart, for they shall see God" (Matthew 5:8). Those words in the Greek can literally be translated, "Happy are the pure in heart, for they and they alone will see God." The first time I realized the meaning of those words, I was a little chagrined. Who is pure? What is the standard?

We've seen how the humble are happy, and how those who are hurting can be happy; but now Jesus comes out and tells us that if we truly want to be happy, we ought to be holy. That's hard to do. I received a letter from a young man recently who told me he had been traveling. Since he was away from his wife, he was thinking about going out to see a pornographic movie; but he turned on the radio instead and heard our program. He wrote to me, explaining how unhappy he was with himself and asking for help. I think that young man represents tens of thousands of men who are involved in ungodly activities and hating themselves for it. Satan tempts us with the lure of pleasure, but those activities always result in unhappiness. Unholy people aren't happy. Sin doesn't ever produce the joy it promises. So Christ says, "If you want to be happy, be holy."

PURITY OF THE HEART

The dictionary says that *purity* is "freedom from foreign mixtures or matter, cleanness, freedom from foulness or dirt, freedom from guilt or defilement." To be pure means that you are living a "clean" life. If you'll look carefully at this passage of Scripture, you'll find that Jesus was very concerned about the lifestyles of the Pharisees. They were pure on the outside, but rotten on the inside. Christ compared them to whitewashed tombs which looked nice outside, but contained rotting corpses on the inside. The Lord criticized them for putting on a display of piety so that they would look good to others while retaining an evil heart. God wants us to be holy throughout, having been cleansed from sin and changed by the Spirit of God. Rather than simply maintaining an outward obedience, the Lord wants us to have an inner holiness with an attitude of love for God and others. We aren't merely to be clean on the outside, but on the inside, in the heart.

The Greeks thought the heart was the center of thinking, so a modern reader could translate the word *heart* for *mind*. In other words, God wants us to have a clean mind, not just go through the motions of doing the right things. In Scripture, the "heart" is always seen as the inside part of a man, the seat of his personality, and the center of his thinking process. Proverbs 23:7 reads, "As he thinks in his heart, so is he." To have a clean heart is to have a clean mind.

When Christ says, "Blessed are the pure in heart," He is encouraging us to have a clean mind before God, not corrupted with evil or impurities. "Keep your heart with all diligence," Solomon says in Proverbs 4:23, "for out of it spring the issues of life." In other words, if you get your heart right, you won't have to worry about the outside. Your actions will follow what your mind is thinking. Godliness doesn't move from the outside in, but from the inside out. If you get your heart right, you'll live a holy life. And one of the benefits of a holy life is the happiness of seeing God.

One of my favorite Old Testament stories is the calling of David. When God called David's predecessor, Saul, to be the king, He chose a tall, handsome, powerful man. Saul looked great on the outside. But Saul had a problem with his heart. He just didn't want to follow God. He routinely violated God's standards until God finally got fed up. Saul was finished. He was not going to be king anymore, nor would his ancestors sit on the throne of Israel. Instead, the Bible says that "the Lord has sought out for himself a man after His own heart" (1 Samuel 13:14). And God selected David.

David wasn't perfect—anyone who has read the man's life knows that. He made a number of mistakes, some of them big. But David had it where it counted: the heart. He was a man after God's own heart. Seeking after the things of God and being willing to obey Him no matter what the cost is to have a heart for God. That's the sort of person Jesus was describing in the Beatitudes.

Purity Portrayed

You may get discouraged as you read about being pure in heart. I've had people say to me, "Pastor, I don't have any hope. No matter how hard I try, I still have the defilement of the world in me. I just can't be pure!" But we have to keep in mind that there are different kinds of purity.

Perfect Purity

First, there is perfect purity, the kind we will one day have in heaven. That's the time we Christians "shall be like Him, for we shall see Him as He is" (1 John 3:2). On that day, every single person who has put his trust in God is going to be one hundred percent pure just as Christ himself is pure. We will be as holy as God. That's perfect purity, but it's out there in the future.

Positional Purity

Second, there is positional purity which is what Christ has done for us through His sacrifice. Remember, God says we have to be holy, but none of us can achieve holiness. If we could, Christ would never have had to come. We are all lost in sin, and it is impossible for any of us to be completely sinless and pure. But God saw mankind's plight, knew we were lost, and sent His Son to earth to show the world what it's like to live a perfect life. Jesus came and died on a cross as a sacrifice to pay the penalty for the sins of all mankind. We can't be pure in our own strength, but if we understand what Christ has done for us and put our trust in Him, He will take away our sins and give us His righteousness. When you have received the righteousness of Jesus Christ, God no longer counts your sin against you. He looks at you and sees that you are positionally pure due to the gracious sacrifice of His Son.

I have put my trust in Christ, so when God looks at me, He sees that my heart is clean. Even though I'm a flawed human being who has failed time after time, God looks down and sees the righteousness of Christ. He accepts me because the righteousness of Christ has been credited to me—I am pure in Jesus. Remember, I'm not pure in David Jeremiah. I am righteous in the Son of God. When the Lord died on that cross, He paid the complete penalty, then imputed His righteousness to me. It's the greatest exchange that has ever taken place; for when God looks at me now, He sees my positional purity. That's why I will one day see God! In the purity of Jesus Christ, I have the guarantee that I will be with Him forever. Not because I'm good, but because His goodness has been granted to me.

Practical Purity

Third, there is practical purity, the everyday living sort of purity. The Bible says that as a Christian I am righteous, so now the Lord expects me to live like the righteous man I have become. Sanctification is being in practice what you already are in position. It is living each day in light of the righteousness of Christ. God wants me pure, but that purity is a challenge. Right now all Christians have positional purity, and some day each of us will have perfect purity, but we seem to have a lot of trouble putting our purity into practice.

THE PATH TO PURITY

To put purity into practice, you've got to have a strategy.

Covenant with Your Eyes

Job 31:1 speaks of making a covenant with your eyes so that as you begin putting purity into practice, you'll commit to watching only pure things. We used to sing a chorus with our children that went like this: "Oh be careful little eyes what you see; oh be careful little eyes what you see; for the Father up above is looking down in love, so be careful little eyes what you see." The eyes are the window to the soul. They are the gate through which most impurity gets into your heart and mind. If there has ever been a time in which Christians needed a covenant with their eyes, it is in this century in America. Everywhere you go there is visual stimuli to steer you away from God. You can't drive down a street or walk through an airport without billboards or television or advertisements flashing something impure. So make a covenant with your eyes regarding what you will gaze at and ponder. Be wary of the books you read, the movies you watch, and the magazines you look at. If you want to develop practical purity, make a covenant with your eyes.

Consecrate Your Mind

Another thing you can do is to consecrate your mind. "As a man thinks in his heart, so is he," the Bible tells us. The heart, according to the Lord Jesus, is the seat of indwelling sin. Evil thoughts, adultery, murder, theft, covetousness, wickedness, and fornication all come from the heart of man. As far back as Noah's time, God perceived that "every intent of the thoughts of his heart was only evil continually" (Genesis 6:5). So we are to focus our minds on good things. "Whatever things are true, whatever things are noble, whatever things are just, whatever things are pure, whatever things are lovely, whatever things are of good report, if there is any virtue and if there is anything praiseworthy, meditate on these things. The things which you learned and received and heard and saw in me, these do, and the God of peace will be with you" (Philippians 4:8–9). Don't fall into the trap of believing you can't control what you think. You may not be able to totally control it, but you can certainly harness it and get it going in the right direction. You can decide not to expose yourself to evil things so that you won't be pondering them.

Commit to Bible Memorization

If you want to begin practicing purity, commit yourself to Bible memory. Find a powerful verse that speaks to some important area of your life, and then keep repeating it to yourself. Think through the verse so that you can remember it without looking it up in your Bible. Memorization is important because you can't always determine when you'll need a thought from God, and you can't always run and get your Bible to find the proper passage that speaks to the need at hand. Hide God's Word in your heart, and it will keep you from sin. When your mind is filled with God's truth, it won't be filled with impurities. Ask the Lord to help you internalize truth so that you can take it out and use it when necessary. "How can a young man cleanse his way?" the psalmist asks; then answers, "By taking heed according to Your word" (Psalm 119:9).

Counteract Satan's Strategy

Christian, learn to counteract Satan's strategy in your life. Satan has a strategy for you just like he does for me. He knows me inside out; he knows everything he can do to upset me or discourage me. He'll use the dumbest things to discourage me, but I've been working to counteract his plan. You see, having a plan is critical to developing practical purity. I once had a man come to me who was struggling with his thought life. He was all right during the day, but he really had a tough time going home. Then he told me that he worked downtown and walked home every day—right through the seedy part of town with adult bookstores and pornography places on either side. He said it was the shortest route home, but I encouraged him to find a longer way. I mean, this guy was struggling in his thought life, but making the same mistake every day. Sometimes all it takes is a little counteraction!

If you're struggling with purity, analyze the enemy. Where does he attack? When? How do the attacks most often begin? Look for ways to fight back. God wants you to be holy because He is holy. He desires you to be like himself. Francois Muriac, a French Canadian writer, has talked openly about his struggles with fleshly temptation. He wanted to be pure, but couldn't find a good reason to support his desire. Marriage didn't cure his lust, self-discipline didn't master it, and repression failed to make it go away. Then he read the words of Jesus in Matthew 5:8: "Blessed are the pure in heart, for they shall see God." In that, he found a reason to be pure. Impurity separates us from God, and Muriac wanted to be close to God. His desire for spiritual intimacy with God became so great in his heart that he would not allow physical impurity to get in the way. If you want to know God, cultivate purity in your life.

APPLICATION

1. Read Exodus 19:10–15.

    a. For what event was Moses preparing the people of Israel? (verse 11)

    b. What were the people to do to prepare to be in God's presence? (verse 10, 14–15)

    c. What was the purpose of their washing their clothes? Was it similar to our dressing up on Sunday? Was it an external symbol of an internal reality?

    d. What was the purpose of abstaining from sexual relations? (verse 15; see Leviticus 15:18)

    e. What is the connection between external purity and internal purity? Can you have one without the other?

    f. Which is most important? Which comes first—that is, which promotes the other?

2. Read Exodus 30:17–21.

    a. What was the bronze laver (basin) for in the tabernacle court? (verse 18)

    b. Who was to use it? (verse 19)

    c. What were they to wash? What did these two body parts symbolize? (verse 19)

    d. When were they to wash? (verse 20)

e. What would happen if they approached the Lord without washing? (verse 20–21)

f. Why was it important for the spiritual leaders—the high priest and his sons—to go through a purification ritual before ministering to the Lord?

3. Read Psalm 51:7–17.
   a. What need did David recognize in his life? (verse 7a)

   b. How does "snow" picture that need? (verse 7b)

   c. What was missing in his life due to impurity? (verses 8, 12)

Happy Are the Holy • 87

d. What kind of heart and spirit was David praying for? (verse 10)

e. What did David promise to do if cleansed from his sin? (verses 13–14)

f. What distinction did David make between external and internal acts of repentance? (verses 16–17)

g. What is the evidence of a true desire for purity? (verse 17)

h. How does a broken spirit and heart lead to a restoration of purity?

    i. How would you combine verse 17 with 1 John 1:9? How do the two verses complement one another?

    j. How does 2 Corinthians 7:9–10 complement verse 17?

4. Read Mark 7:1–23.

    a. What traditions did the Pharisees practice in Jesus' day? (verses 3–4)

    b. How did Jesus' disciples violate those traditions? (verses 1–2)

    c. When the Pharisees questioned Jesus about the disciples' practices, how did Jesus respond? Who had the real problem—the Pharisees or the disciples? (verse 6–7)

d. Explain verses 8–13. What is Jesus illustrating for them? (verse 8).

e. What principle did Jesus give concerning purity? (verses 15–19)

f. What kinds of things coming from inside a person make him truly impure in God's sight? (verses 20–23).

DID YOU KNOW?

In the Old Testament, the Mosaic Law required ceremonial purification in four situations: (1) the birth of a child, accomplished through circumcision of a male child and isolation of the mother for a time (Leviticus 12:2 ff.); (2) contact with a corpse (Numbers 19:1–13); (3) certain diseases such as leprosy (Leviticus 13:8 ff.); and (4) uncleanness due to bodily discharges (Leviticus 15). Family purity was maintained by strict regulations regarding sexual practices (Leviticus 20:10–21; Deuteronomy 22:13–30). In the New Testament, purity is still required though the emphasis shifts from the external to the internal (Mark 7:14–16; 1 Corinthians 5:9–13). (*NIV Compact Dictionary of the Bible*, "purification.")

LESSON 8

HAPPY ARE THE HEALERS

Matthew 5:9

In this lesson we learn how to manifest God's peace in the world.

OUTLINE

The League of Nations was formed in 1920, and the United Nations in 1945, to promote peace among the nations of the world. Unfortunately, the cause of unrest and war is not nations, but the nature of man. Only God's peace can settle the wars in the human heart.

I. **What the Bible Says About Peace**
    A. Peace *with* God
    B. Peace *of* God
    C. Peace *from* God

II. **What the Bible Says About Peacemakers**
    A. What Peacemakers Do
    B. Where Peacemakers Are Needed

OVERVIEW

"Blessed are the peacemakers, for they shall be called sons of God" (Matthew 5:9). Humanity's quest for peace has been illustrated throughout the years by architecture. The *Statue of Liberty* offers a gesture of peace to those who come to our shores. The *Statue of Shalom* in Israel looks over the harbor at Haifa to remind people that there is another way. In front of Tokyo Station is the statue of a man with his arms outstretched to heaven, while underneath is the Greek word *agape*—love. In almost every part of the world, you can find some symbolic representation of man's quest for peace. Yet for all our labors, there is little peace in the world.

What the Bible Says about Peace

The problem is not with nations, but with the nature of man. As long as man remains separated from God and refuses to follow His divine plan for life, he will never be able to know any true peace. Man keeps trying with peace treaties and ambassadors and the United Nations peace-keeping forces, but it all proves to be awfully frustrating. While peace is being talked about on one front, a war breaks out on another. "But the wicked are like the troubled sea, when it cannot rest, whose waters cast up mire and dirt. There is no peace," says my God, "for the wicked" (Isaiah 57:20–21). As long as he determines in his heart to have none of God, he cannot have peace. He cannot have it individually, corporately, in his family, or in his country. He will not know peace until things are straightened out in his heart with God. We were created by God. Only He has the plan, for He put all things together. God alone knows what brings peace, and He says that until we accept the Prince of Peace, there isn't any chance of getting out of the war zone. So we fight at home, at work, at church, and among nations—all because we don't have peace.

God's Word tells us about the nature of peace and describes at least three kinds of peace.

Peace with *God*

In Romans 5:1, Paul says, "Therefore, having been justified by faith, we have peace with God through our Lord Jesus Christ." God is not my enemy, though I've been at war with Him since I was born. My old depraved nature is at war with God. We are not born good and then go bad, as some think. Scripture is clear that man is born in sin. Children come into this world screaming for their own way, at war with God. But while we were at war with Him, He sent His only Son, Jesus Christ, into this world. He paid the penalty for all our sins when He died on the cross; so now the war is over. We can have peace with God through Jesus Christ.

When I explain the Gospel to people and they accept Christ into their lives, they often talk about having peace with God. Their war with God has been brought to an end. Without peace with God, we can never be peacemakers. We have no peace, so we cannot share it with anyone else. We can't give away what we don't have. In order to become peacemakers, we must have peace with God. That means coming to terms with what Christ has done on the Cross, taking away our sins and creating a relationship between us and God. When we became Christians, we were given peace with God.

Peace of *God*

Many Christians have peace with God, but don't have the peace of God. That's why Christian bookstores are filled with so many self-help books. When I go into a bookstore, I see all these books about how we can straighten out our lives; and it makes me wonder what message they send to non-Christians. It would seem we really don't have our lives together. Why is it that so many Christians who have peace with God never get to the place of having the peace of God in their lives?

In John 14:27, the Lord Jesus said to His disciples, "Peace I leave with you, My peace I give to you; not as the world gives do I give to you. Let not your heart be troubled, neither let it be afraid." Christ wanted His people to have peace in their lives, no matter what they were facing. Without His peace, we're a troubled lot. He wants to give us the very peace of God. Do you have the inner calmness, the quiet assurance within you that all is well? Can you say with the psalmist, "I will both lie down in peace, and sleep; for You alone, O Lord, make me dwell in safety"? (4:8) Can you remain peaceful in the face of chaotic circumstances? We all live in a war zone. Our neighborhoods face terrible troubles, there is great financial strain, and we struggle with job-related tensions. But if you have the peace of God, you can rest in peace.

Peace from *God*

There is a third kind of peace that we experience when facing a major decision. God doesn't have a magic instruction book where you can turn to a particular page to discover His answer to your question. Instead, His book offers timeless principles that draw His people to himself. As we begin to fill our minds with His principles, things become clear. He has already given us several clear "thou shalt nots" and some "thou shalts," so where we sometimes get stumped is in the gray areas where we must judge between what is good and what is best. The choices may look equally acceptable, so we need the peace of God to guide us.

Colossians 3:15 reads, "Let the peace of God rule in your hearts," and that verse offers some great advice for deciding a course of action. After we have read our Bible and talked to Christian friends about our choices, we can ask the Lord to give us peace about our decision. It's okay to pray, "Lord, I don't know what to do in this situation, so I'm going to go this way. Please give me your peace." God can give us His peace in the major decisions of our lives after we've exhausted our ability to study the principles. Sometimes we just know in our hearts which choice is correct. When I was pastoring in Fort Wayne, Indiana, I was asked to pastor a church in California. Both churches were great situations, and I really didn't know what to do. I'd make up my mind one way, then change it the next day. Finally I told the Lord, "I think I'm supposed to go to California. Please give me a peace about my decision." And He did. I've never again doubted that it was the right decision because I've experienced the peace of God.

What the Bible Says About Peacemakers

Christ says that those with peace will be happy—blissful, joy-filled, ecstatic people. They know in their hearts that they are at peace with God. They have a certainty that they are no longer under condemnation, but have been set free from sin. They are righteous in the eyes of God, and that allows them to become peacemakers. The man or woman who has peace can help other people find peace with God. In one sense, a peacemaker is an evangelist because he goes about finding people at war with God and sharing the peace of Christ with them. Whenever I preach the Gospel and tell people how to know Jesus Christ, I have functioned as a peacemaker. If you are sharing your faith with others, you have become a peacemaker; and the Bible says there is great joy in being a peacemaker. For me, the greatest joy I've ever known has been introducing other people to the Lord Jesus. It's the most wonderful experience you can have. If you're not sharing your faith, you are missing a great blessing.

What Peacemakers Do

Peacemakers bring unity between men and God, and they also bring unity between men and other men. Bringing estranged people together is a blessing. Eugene Peterson, in his book *The Message*, translates Matthew 5:9 this way: "You're blessed when you can show people how to cooperate instead of compete or fight. That's when you discover who you really are, and your place in God's family." That's why Jesus warned us to reconcile with other people before coming to worship Him. We need to be at peace with men to really experience the blessing of peace with God. Whether or not we are the ones at fault, we are called by God to make peace before we can truly worship Him. Happy is the man who helps put things back together.

Where Peacemakers Are Needed

With all the unhappiness and violence in our homes, we need peacemakers. I believe many Christian counselors are serving exactly that function, bringing peace to troubled families. Too many Christian marriages are falling apart, and we need godly men and women who can sit down with couples and help them reconcile and find peace. We need peacemakers in our communities, bringing reconciliation between races. We need peacemakers in the international community, bringing peace to warring nations. We even need peacemakers in the church, bringing reconciliation between churches and denominations, and sometimes even among church members. I've seen people get into serious disputes over the church organ, the carpet, the elders, the choir, and the pastor. Billy Graham has noted that Mary and Joseph lost the young boy Jesus in church one day, and in the same way too many Christians have lost Jesus in the church. They've become so busy arguing about church stuff that they've lost Christ in the process. "As much as depends on you," Paul tells the Roman Christians, "live peaceably with all men" (Romans 12:18). In other words, if there isn't a moral issue or doctrinal dispute, be a peacemaker, not a war-monger.

I read about two deacons who had been quarreling over an old fence that lay between their houses. They argued so much, the two men eventually stopped talking to one another. But then one of them, wanting to make peace, brought his Bible to that fence and asked his brother to read it while he prayed. "I can't read," the man said, "I forgot my glasses." So the first man suggested, "Here, use mine." As they read the Bible and prayed together, those two men found peace. As the one man handed back the other's glasses, he said, "You know, that old fence really looks different through your glasses." That's exactly what a peacemaker does. He sees through the eyes of the other person to bring them together. When we have peace with God, we can learn to see things from God's perspective and become a peacemaker.

When the walls of communism fell in that wonderful summer of 1989, the church was at the core of the peacemaking. As the tanks of Poland, Hungary, East Germany, Czechoslovakia, Bulgaria, Romania, Russia, and Yugoslavia rolled into the cities, they were met by crowds of people on their knees, praying. Half a billion people threw off the yoke of oppression with very little violence. The Christians led the way as peacemakers, praying and singing songs, and the lie that was communism came to an end. The joy and excitement that filled the people was a wonder to behold as decades of war came to an end. The peacemakers reflect the peace of God to the world. It's obvious to everyone. "Blessed are the peacemakers, for they shall be called sons of God."

APPLICATION

1. Read Matthew 10:34–39.

    a. What surprising statement does Jesus make in verse 34?

    b. Compare His words in light of Isaiah's words in Isaiah 9:6.

    c. What kind of unrest did Jesus come to earth to promote? (verses 35–36)

    d. How does Jesus explain his words in verse 37–39?

    e. So, is Jesus really anti-peace in this passage, or is He talking about the likely outcome of responses to the Gospel?

    f. Which is God more interested in—His truth or people's feelings?

Happy Are the Healers • 97

g. If everyone in a family responded positively to the Gospel, would there be peace?

h. If there is not peace, whose responsibility is it—God's or man's?

i. So, has Jesus brought unrest to the world, or has His gospel simply revealed the ungodliness in the hearts of men?

j. Verses 35–36 are a quotation from Micah 7:6. What was happening in that setting that was turning family members against one another?

k. When the truth or judgment of God enters, what can it be expected to produce before it produces peace?

2. Read Jeremiah 6:11–15.

   a. Who was dealing falsely with the people of Israel? (verse 13)

   b. How were they dealing falsely? (verse 14)

   c. How did their false words help "slightly?" (verse 14)

   d. What is the difference between counterfeit peace and true peace?

   e. Evaluate this statement by the late theologian Francis Schaeffer: "If America ever falls, it won't because of a military invasion. It will be as a result of citizens yielding to whomever will promise to maintain their personal peace and affluence."

Happy Are the Healers • 99

f. Evaluate this statement: "Peace at any price."

g. When does the price for peace get too high?

3. Read Luke 19:41–44.
   a. Why did Jesus weep over Jerusalem? (verse 41; cf. Matthew 9:36)

   b. What had the Jews not seen that would have brought them peace? (verse 42)

   c. Who or what had visited the Jews that they missed? (verse 44)

   d. What kind of peace did Jesus offer them? (John 14:27)

4. How do we obtain peace with God? (Romans 5:1)

   a. How does being spiritually minded bring peace? (Romans 8:6)

   b. How is Romans 14:19 a good definition of a "peacemaker"?

   c. How can you tell when the kingdom of God is present? (Romans 14:17)

   d. To what extent is any person responsible for bringing peace? (Romans 12:18)

Happy Are the Healers

5. Define the following . . .

   a. Peace with God

   b. Peace of God

   c. Peace from God

DID YOU KNOW?

In the Old Testament, the Hebrew word for peace (*shalom*) was replete with illustrations of its meaning. *Shalom* was derived from the verb that meant "to complete" or "make sound, or whole." The verb was used to describe the completion of the temple (1 Kings 7:51) and the wall around Jerusalem (Nehemiah 6:15), the repayment of debt (Jeremiah 16:18), and restoration (Leviticus 6:5). The root word *s-l-m* was used as a greeting, meaning "are you well?" or "are you whole, content, tranquil?" (Genesis 29:6). The word gradually came to be translated as *peace* as it was used to define the absence of war (Judges 4:17), and the reign of the coming Messiah (Isaiah 2:2–4; 9:2–7).

LESSON 9

HAPPY ARE THE HARASSED

Matthew 5:10–12

In this lesson we learn how persecution for Christ's sake leads to rewards from God.

OUTLINE

Many Western Christians believe that the persecution of the church is something to study in history books. Not true. The Christian church is the most persecuted religious body in the modern world. Jesus' promise of rewards for the persecuted church still applies today.

I. The Reason for Persecution

II. The Realities of Persecution
    A. The Bad News
        1. They will revile you
        2. They will persecute you
        3. They will harass you
    B. The Good News
        1. Persecution is a compliment
        2. Persecution is a credential
        3. Persecution is a catalyst
        4. Persecution is a criterion

OVERVIEW

Blessed are those who are persecuted for righteousness' sake, for theirs is the kingdom of heaven. Blessed are you when they revile and persecute you, and say all kinds of evil against you falsely for My sake. Rejoice and be exceedingly glad, for great is your reward in heaven, for so they persecuted the prophets who were before you" (Matthew 5:10–12).

Jenny Adams serves in Peru as a missionary with Baptist Mid-Missions. She has been there for thrity-four years, ministering faithfully as a teacher at the mission's Bible school and in several remote villages. She drove her own van and often gave passengers rides into town. One day she offered a ride to a young woman who had previously attended the mission school, the daughter of a village pastor. Little did Miss Adams know that this young woman's brother was a cocaine processor who frequently used his sister to transport the drugs. Miss Adams was arrested with more than three kilos of cocaine in her vehicle, and under Peruvian law a person is guilty until proven innocent. In her case, the press was quick to exploit the story to discredit foreign missionaries. The newspapers dubbed her "the cocaine missionary," and her long years of service were ignored. After twenty days of imprisonment, Jenny Adams was released, but not until the work of her mission had suffered from false witnesses. She was innocent of all charges, but that didn't matter. She was persecuted anyway.

Nobody wants to be persecuted, and it doesn't seem natural to find happiness in persecution. Everybody I know wants to be liked and wants to get along with others, so it's really hard to understand how anyone could find blessing in being persecuted. As a matter of fact, it seems like Christians should be complimented for their extraordinary behavior, not vilified for their faith. It would seem reasonable to think that others would respect our lifestyle, even if they didn't agree with it. Yet in this world, that's not how it happens. Good people are persecuted in this life.

Second Timothy 3:12 says, "Yes, and all who desire to live godly in Christ Jesus will suffer persecution." We ought to expect persecution. Christ was persecuted, and so were His disciples. They turned the world upside down everywhere they went, causing an uproar because their values and faith were in complete contradiction to a world lost in sin. Everyone who tries to live for Jesus in this world can expect opposition.

The Reason for Persecution

The kind of persecution we're talking about is that which occurs "for righteousness' sake," the kind that comes from having your life identified with Jesus Christ. We shouldn't assume that everything bad that happens to us is persecution. Sometimes our own stress, sin, or bad choices can bring difficulties into our lives. First Peter 4:15 reads, "Let none of you suffer as a murderer, a thief, an evildoer, or as a busybody in other people's matters." We can get into a lot of trouble just by doing the wrong things, but that doesn't make it persecution. If we are in trouble for doing something wrong, we have no business taking the blessing of Matthew 5:10 to heart.

To be persecuted for righteousness' sake means that we are hated or opposed solely for being a follower of Christ. When we are doing what is right and living for God, yet suffer because of it, that is persecution. Some feel it on the job, some are faced with it in school, and some of us have run into it in social and civic situations. This world belongs to Satan, is at war with God, and attacks Christians because they represent God in the world. We become the social conscience of the environment in which we live. Sometimes we don't have to say a thing; we can just walk around and be different. People don't like those who are different; they want us to be like them.

When I was a student in seminary, I worked for the Illinois-California Express as a dock hand. I worked from three until eight every day, loading freight trucks and lacing tires. I'd throw tires up into the truck and then lace them so they'd stay put. It was the dirtiest job in the business, but I worked with some guys who came in white T-shirts and never got them sweaty or soiled. That was no way for a Christian to work, so I ignored them and simply started throwing tires left and right. I had rubber all over my clothes, sweat pouring down my face, and tires all around me. Then one day the union steward came down to my end of the dock and said, "Son, you've got to quit what you're doing." When I asked him what he meant, he said to me, "You can't work like you're working. You're showing us up. You'd better quit or you're going to have a lot of trouble here."

Now I was just putting in an honest day's work, and I discovered that if you work hard, the time goes faster. I didn't want to spend my day sitting around trying to figure out how to get my job done! So I did my job with all my heart. I didn't say anything or offer any words of criticism to the others, I just worked the way I thought was honoring to God. But I found out about persecution. Nobody would sit with me in the lunch room. No one would talk with me on the job. I was persecuted for righteousness' sake.

THE REALITIES OF PERSECUTION

The Bad News

Jesus describes how persecution will occur by using three different words. Christians will be reviled, persecuted, and harassed.

They will revile you. First, He says you will be reviled. That word literally means to throw things into your face. For example, when Christ was hanging on the cross, some of those in attendance made fun of Him, mocking Him with vile, malicious words. We can't just expect to be chased out of the groups of which we are a part; we will also be subject to evil words and scorn. People will say bad things about us, just as they did about Christ. If we live for Jesus, we can't expect that non-Christians are going to understand us or accept us.

They will persecute you. The second term Christ uses is persecute. In other words, they will come after us because we are good and they are evil, and evil hates good. Persecution has been around since the fall of man. Cain killed Abel because his own works were evil but his brother's righteous. Joseph was persecuted because his father loved him. Moses was reviled, Samuel rejected, Elijah despised, and Nehemiah oppressed. Jesus Christ, the faithful witness of His Father, was put to death by the people to whom He came to minister. Stephen was stoned for speaking the truth, John and Peter were cast into prison, and James was beheaded for preaching the Good News of the kingdom. Every one of the apostles was martyred for his faith except for John who was exiled to the Isle of Patmos. Why did God's people suffer such persecution? Because they were doing right.

Where did we ever get the idea that things will work out just fine if we do everything right? The Bible says exactly the opposite. I still remember the day my teenage son came up to me and said, "Dad, I just learned something. Life isn't fair." What a hard but wonderful truth! God never said life would be fair.

They will harass you. The third phrase Jesus used to describe the harassment of His people was that people would "say all kinds of evil against you falsely." Have you ever noticed how creative people can get when they're trying to make up lies about Christians?

Modern entertainment seems to go out of its way to portray pastors and Christians in the ugliest way possible. Even in the church, I've marvelled at the creative ability some have to say mean things. I once told a story on my radio program about helping my son put toilet paper on someone's house because she had been terrorizing us for three weeks. Within days I received a three-page letter from somebody telling me what a bad guy I was for pushing that idea, and how we could have used the money that bought the toilet paper to help missionaries, and how he had met with the staff at his church and warned them never to do anything like toilet-papering a house! I encouraged the man to lighten up. Life is serious enough without spending our time trying to make someone else's life miserable.

The Good News

As Christians, we've got to expect persecution. If we live for God in this world, it will come. We don't always have control over our situation, but we do have control over our response to it. We can't determine what action will occur, but we can determine what our attitude will be. Christ says that our attitude should be one of happiness. We are to rejoice in persecution. We're to be exceedingly glad. That may sound like it doesn't make sense, but the fact is that persecution brings rewards in which we can rejoice.

Persecution is a compliment. To persecute someone is to show that you take him so seriously that you believe he needs to be eliminated. No one persecutes an ineffective individual. Persecution only comes to the person whose life is so positive and effective that our fallen world considers him dangerous. George Bernard Shaw once said that the finest compliment the world can pay an author is to burn his books. Those books must be powerful to raise the hackles of the world.

I once saw a film about a football player whose coach was always on him. Every time he turned around, the coach was barking at him about something. When the player finally complained, the coach told him, "Son, thank the Lord I'm after you. I don't have any plans for all those other guys I don't yell at. But I'm on your case because you've got potential. And I'm going to stay on your case until you fulfill the potential I see in you." Persecution is a compliment. It's a way of showing us that we're being effective, that we've attracted the attention of Satan, that what we're doing is so powerful the enemy wants to eliminate us.

Persecution is a credential. When we are persecuted for righteousness' sake, it is proof that we're on the right side. Christ once told His disciples, "You will be hated by all for My name's sake. But he who endures to the end will be saved" (Matthew 10:22). Jesus Christ is a King in exile. We who are His followers are identified with Him and looked down upon because we are like Him. The Lord was persecuted by a world that didn't understand Him and, as His followers, we can expect the same persecution.

Matthew tells us that the prophets got this same treatment. Throughout history, everyone who has been unafraid to stand up and be counted for Christ has taken flak. It is a witness that we are living for Christ in a world that doesn't know Him.

I preach every Sunday, and I love to talk about the good and positive things in the Bible. But the Word of God also has some hard things to say. When I come across those hard things, I will often think to myself, "Lord, do I really need to preach that?! I'd rather not." But I do, since the Bible is God's revelation to us. And when I preach those hard things, I invariably get notes from people who don't like hearing them. Sometimes people will leave the service because they don't like what is being said. I've been criticized for being too clear about the truth. But what option do I have? I can either preach the whole truth and be obedient to God, or I can compromise and make everybody comfortable. God hasn't called me to preach only the "nice" parts of Scripture, but the entire message of God.

We all face moments like that. Perhaps it's at a business meeting when they bring out the glasses and call for a round of drinks. Your response to your client might make a difference in whether or not you get the deal. You have to make a decision, and it could cost you the client. But to participate in something you believe to be wrong can cost you your clear conscience and the Lord's blessing on your life. When you are persecuted, you are identified with Jesus Christ.

Persecution is a catalyst. The Bible says that when we suffer for righteousness, we experience growth. The best lessons are the ones we learn in hard times. Most of us really don't learn very well from prosperity and good times. I've learned my most valuable lessons and grown the most in my walk with Christ when I have experienced pain and difficulties. "We also glory in tribulations," Paul says in Romans 5:3–5, "knowing that tribulation produces perseverance; and perseverance, character; and character, hope. Now hope does not disappoint, because the love of God has been poured out in our hearts by the Holy Spirit who was given to us."

Nobody enjoys going through hard times, but we always look back and know that it was those difficulties that caused us to grow.

If you are having stress at work or at school, and you are trying to do right, keep track of what God is teaching you in the process. Don't forget those lessons, for the Lord is shaping you into a more mature Christian, building Christlikeness into your life.

Persecution is a criterion. Jesus tells us to rejoice in persecution, for "great is your reward in heaven." Persecution is a condition, a criterion for something better God has in store for those who love Him. "If indeed we suffer with Him," it says in Romans 8:17, "that we may also be glorified together." To suffer persecution is to be an eventual partaker of joy.

"If we endure," Paul told Timothy, "we shall also reign with Him" (2 Timothy 2:12). There is something involved in persecution that identifies us with Jesus Christ and is the criterion for blessing here on earth and in eternity. In the process of being God's person, we start to find persecution happening to us. Remember that the persecuted are happy because they are being prepared for heaven.

Persecution is one of the natural consequences of living the Christian life. It is to the Christian what growing pains are to a child. No persecution, no reward. No suffering, no glory. No struggle, no victory. First Peter 5:10 asks that the God of all grace "who called us to His eternal glory by Christ Jesus, after you have suffered a while, perfect, establish, strengthen, and settle you." God wants to make a difference in our world through your life.

APPLICATION

1. Read Genesis 39:1–23.

   a. What temptation was placed before Joseph in Egypt? (verse 12)

   b. What was Joseph's response to the temptation? (verse 12)

   c. How was Joseph wrongly accused? (verses 13–18)

   d. How was Joseph persecuted? (verse 20)

   e. How was Joseph rewarded by God for his faithfulness? (verses 21–23)

   f. How do we know Joseph's refusal was done for God and not just out of a sense of morality? (verse 9)

   g. What is there in Matthew 5:11 that carefully defines the kind of persecution that God rewards?

2. Read Acts 6:8–7:1, 54–60.

   a. By what was Stephen's ministry characterized? (verse 6:8)

   b. Who opposed his ministry? (verse 6:9)

   c. How was Stephen falsely accused by his opponents? (verses 6:11, 13–14)

   d. How was he persecuted? (verse 6:12)

   e. How did Stephen respond to the charges brought against him? (verse 7:1; survey 7:2–53)

   f. How did Stephen's persecution end? (verses 7:57–58)

   g. How was Stephen rewarded for his faithfulness even before he arrived in heaven? (verse 7:55–56)

3. Describe at least three ways that Christians in America can be persecuted for the sake of Christ, and what the Christian's response should be:

   a.

   b.

   c.

4. Read Hebrews 11:32–40.

   a. Jesus said the "prophets who were before you" were persecuted for God's sake (Matthew 5:12). List all the ways they suffered and were persecuted. (verses 32–38)

5. Read 1 Peter 2:18–25.

   a. What does Peter say is commendable? (verses 19–20)

   b. What does "conscience toward God" mean in terms of the reasons one suffers? (verse 19)

   c. What if we suffer because of our own choices or sin? How does God respond? (verse 20)

   d. What did Christ do when He suffered for the sake of obedience toward God? To whom did He entrust His future? (verse 23)

   e. What does verse 21 say about how we should respond to Christ's way of suffering?

f. If God "judges righteously" (verse 23), what does that say about how you can entrust yourself to Him?

g. If you have suffered for the sake of Christ in this life with no recompense being offered, what do you expect God will do for you in heaven?

6. In the spirit of Matthew 5:11–12, compose a prayer for those Christians who are suffering around the world for the sake of Christ, that they may have grace to endure until they are rewarded in heaven.

DID YOU KNOW?

Open Doors, a ministry dedicated to serving the persecuted Christian church worldwide, estimates that 200 million Christians in the world are regularly interrogated, arrested, or killed because of their faith in Christ. Another 200 to 400 million Christians face discrimination or alienation because of their faith. In North Korea, one of the most religiously repressive countries on earth, thousands of Christians are held in labor camps and 400,000 are forced to worship secretly. Churches and mission organizations around the world unite annually in November for the International Day of Prayer for the Persecuted Church (IDOP).

LESSON 10

HOW TO REALLY BE HAPPY

Matthew 5:1–12

In this lesson we discover that true happiness is found by defeating the world with the Word.

OUTLINE

The recipes for finding happiness in this world are innumerable. Ask a thousand people, and you'll get a thousand different strategies. Since we were not made to live in a fallen world, true happiness must be found outside it—through the living and written Word.

I. How to Be Happy—The Principles

II. How to Be Happy—The Practice
   A. Understand the Aggressive Pull of the World on Your Life
      1. The progression of the world
      2. The pull of the world
      3. The permanence of the world
   B. Undertake an Aggressive Program in the Word

OVERVIEW

I read a book recently with the theory that the two greatest revolutions in this century were the communist revolution, now dead, and the Freudian revolution, now stronger than ever. Every year more than $4 billion go into counseling in this country as Americans seek to solve the riddle of their unhappiness. Psychology is no longer the province of some arcane theorizing by European intellectuals or a luxury available only to those who have enough money to buy professional consolation for their troubled egos. Nowadays everybody is either in recovery or in denial. We're all rehabilitating our psyches, getting in touch with our inner child, and joining support groups to talk about our depressions, anxieties, compulsions, neuroses, and search for self-esteem.

The fact is, what we're trying to do in this country is to find happiness. The things we thought would make us happy haven't worked, so people are heading by the thousands to counselors to find out why. It is estimated that eighty million Americans will see a counselor next year, and thousands of people will start new careers as counselors. The search for happiness has caused a boom in the counseling industry.

HOW TO BE HAPPY—THE PRINCIPLES

Not long ago, ABC television ran a special called "The Mystery of Happiness." They went to those we would normally expect to be happy to find out if achieving their dream had changed their lives. For example, they asked a woman who had won $26 million in a lottery if she was happy. "Not really," was her response. They asked European royalty and Pulitzer Prize winners if they were happy, but they weren't. They even talked with sports stars, but most of them could only talk about their dissatisfaction with their contracts. One guy, the quarterback of a Super Bowl winning team, said that after winning the big game, all he could think of was, "Is this all there is?"

I was amazed that non-Christians put this together, since the entire program pointed out the unhappiness of man. About all they could do was reveal how babies get happy when they get what they want and become unhappy when we take things away. But anybody can find out what God says will make mankind happy—just read Matthew chapter five. Jesus says to us that we won't find happiness in the things of the world. We can devote our lives to pleasure, accomplishment, fame, money, or anything else that the world values and promotes, but those things won't make us happy. Instead, Christ offers a series of startling messages on how to be happy, stating things in complete opposition to what the world says will make us happy.

Happy are the *humble.* The world tells us not to be humble. We need to be self-assertive, make sure everybody knows how good we are, and tell our story. The world suggests we even brag a little so that we'll get noticed. But Jesus says that it will be the humble who inherit the kingdom of heaven. God will resist the proud and exalt the humble. He will draw near to those who recognize that they are incomplete apart from God.

Happy are the *hurting.* The world says to avoid pain at all costs. Whatever we have to do to get rid of pain, we should do it. Cover it up, ignore it, mask it, or pretend it's not there because we want to stay away from pain. But Jesus says that the most profound experiences we ever have will come from pain. The greatest truths will be learned through suffering. Some of our most joyous moments will be when everything on the outside is dictating anguish in our lives. Happy are those who hurt, for they shall be comforted.

Happy are the *harnessed.* The world says that we can have it all. If we've got power, we ought to use it. Take every resource to the limit and grab for all the gusto we can. But Jesus says that real happiness is when your power is controlled by the Spirit of God. Joy comes in knowing we have power, but it is under control. We don't have to demonstrate power continually regardless of the world's expectations.

Happy are the *hungry.* The world says that we don't want to be hungry; we want to be satisfied. We don't want to have anything lacking in our lives since that's a sign of not being successful, so we need to get everything we can. We should gorge ourselves on things. We should drive ourselves to be successful in today's world. But Jesus says that true joy can never be found in material things. Happiness comes from having an inner desire to know God and partake of His nature. Those people who fill themselves up on the Lord, rather than the world, will find real happiness.

Happy are the *helpers.* The world says that happiness is being served by others. The world is a triangle; and when we get to the top, everyone below us will serve us. So we should do everything in our power to get above others. But Jesus says that He came into this world not to be served, but to serve. He came to give His life away. Happiness is found in serving others, not in being served. If you want to be great in God's kingdom, learn to be the servant of all. Happy are those who are merciful to others, for they shall be ministered to.

Happy are the *holy*. The world says that joy is found in unrestrained freedom. Sex, drugs, and any pleasurable experience are lifted up as the ultimate goal and glorified as hallmarks of "freedom." Perversions are marched down Main Street in the name of free speech. This is supposed to give us a sense that we control our own destiny, that we can make our existence happy through the indulgence of sinful delights. But Jesus says that holy people are the ones who are truly happy. I've been a pastor for more than thirty years, and I've yet to meet a happy adulterer. We don't find joy through unrestrained passion. Happiness comes from having a clean heart and knowing that we are walking close to the Almighty.

Happy are the *healers*. The world says that we are in competition with our fellow workers and should build competitions, use politics, beat people, knock each other out, and climb over the carnage to get to the top. But Jesus says that the happy people are the peacemakers, those who can heal situations rather than exacerbate them. Find people who are hurting and heal them. If you've got a problem with a colleague, mend it. Rather than dividing people, unite them. Happiness is found not in creating war, but in establishing peace.

Happy are the *harassed*. The world wants us to conform to its image. It wants us to live by its standards. It is at war with God, and expects us to be, too. If we decide to stand with God, they'll attack us. They'll say bad things about us, harass us, and try to ruin our reputations. But Jesus says we ought to be happy when persecution comes, for it is a sign that we belong to God. We can be happy in the face of harassment; for we know that our lives must be making an impact, or the devil wouldn't bother with us.

As I look over Christ's design for happiness, I'm struck by the fact that it isn't the list I would have created. This wouldn't be the formula for happiness that I would have suggested. But these are exactly the things that will bring happiness. The world is in direct opposition to God, so God's formula for success is directly opposite to the world's. We can have the blessing and benediction of God if we'll follow these principles.

How to Be Happy—The Practice

The Christian life isn't easy. Just knowing the Beatitudes will not make us happy. We live in this world, but we aren't of the world. So while we're living in this culture, we have to learn how to live God's way; and that will create tension with our world.

Understand the Aggressive Pull of the World on Your Life

Psalm 1 helps describe how we can live God's way: "Blessed is the man who walks not in the counsel of the ungodly, nor stands in the path of sinners, nor sits in the seat of the scornful" (verse 1). There are three things to notice in that verse.

The progression of the world – There are people in this world who are ungodly; that is, they live life without God. They aren't going in any direction; they simply don't have God in their lives. The next step away from God is toward sin, and the psalmist says that there are people in the world who are sinners, overtly acting in opposition to God's truth. The third sort of people are the scornful, those who are rebellious against God and blasphemous in their attitude toward Him. As a person is pulled into the world, he is pulled away from God and toward sin and rebellion.

The pull of the world – Notice that the writer uses three words to describe the world's pull on us. First he talks about those who listen to the counsel of the ungodly, getting information from those who have no knowledge of God. Second, he speaks of the path of sinners, which is when we start following a path away from God. Third, he tells of the seat of sinners, those who have grown completely comfortable in their lives apart from God. If a man will look back over his life, he'll find that the things with which he used to be uncomfortable have gradually become comfortable to him. That's the pull of the world.

The permanence of the world – The author of the psalm says we first walk or associate with those separated from God. Then we stand with sinners, identifying ourselves with them. Finally we sit with the scoffers, making their lifestyle our own. This is the pattern of our world, and it's sucking Christians into it every day. Jesus stepped into this system and said, "I don't want My people to live like that in the world. Here is God's alternative." Then He explained how we can find happiness. By living out the Beatitudes, we can experience the life-changing power of God in the midst of an evil culture.

Undertake an Aggressive Program in the Word

The only way to survive in a world which tries to slowly poison our minds is to renew our minds each day. The psalmist says in Psalm 1 that the blessed man is the one who delights in the law of the Lord, meditating on it day and night. When I open my Bible for personal devotions, I know that I'm looking at the very Word of God. It's different from everything else around me. What I'm reading is in a whole different universe. I'm getting a transfusion of heavenly culture into my system. I know that if I try to make it in this world, I'll get pulled down. I'll never be happy following the world's plan.

But when I came to Jesus Christ, the happiness of this world was ruined for me. I've got the Holy Spirit inside me, and I can never be happy unless I'm walking with Him. People can try to be happy, but they'll never achieve it apart from the Lord. Christians can try to follow the world's plan for happiness, but the only way to find it is to let the Word of God cleanse and renew them.

Paul said to the Christians in Rome, "I beseech you therefore, brethren, by the mercies of God, that you present your bodies a living sacrifice, holy, acceptable to God, which is your reasonable service. And do not be conformed to this world, but be transformed by the renewing of your mind" (Romans 12:1–2). By allowing God's Word to refresh and transform you, you can begin to see the principles of Jesus Christ start to work in your life. You'll be blessed—happy. There is a path to happiness the world knows nothing about. If we spend our lives cultivating the Word of God, we'll find real happiness.

APPLICATION

1. Read 1 John 2:15–17.

   a. What is the basic command of this passage? (verse 15)

   b. What does this command suggest about the possibility of blessing in this world? Would God command us not to pursue something that would make us truly blessed?

   c. "If anyone loves" is in the subjunctive mood in Greek—the mood of choice or possibility. What does this Greek construction imply about responsibility?

   d. How does the second half of verse 15 parallel Matthew 6:24?

   e. What three aspects of the world is fallen human nature most attracted to? (verse 16)

   • the lust of the _____

   • the lust of the _____

   • the pride of _____

f. What relationship do these three things have with God? (verse 16)

g. If these three are not from God, how much potential is there for finding true happiness in them?

h. If these are not from God, who are they from? (1 John 5:19)

i. What will ultimately happen to these counterfeit objects of desire? (2:17a)

j. What will happen to those who pursue God instead of pursuing the lusts of this world? (verse 17b)

k. Where do you want to be found at the end of this age—passing away with the world or abiding forever with God?

1. How much certainty do you have as to where you will be? Explain the basis of your certainty.

2. Read Philippians 4:4–9.

    a. What is to characterize the Christian on a continual basis? (verse 4)

    b. What does that mean to you? What does a joyful Christian "look like?"

    c. What does a joyful Christian "look like" in times of adversity? Does being joyful mean denying reality?

    d. Connect verse 6 with 1 John 2:16. If you are tempted to pursue the lusts of this world, what should you do?

    e. What result does God promise when you seek Him instead of the things of this world? (Philippians 4:7)

How to Really Be Happy

f. Instead of pursuing the lusts of this world, explain what you think Paul is suggesting in verses 8–9 as worthy objects of our passion in this world—things that are . . .

- true

- noble

- just

- pure

- beautiful (*BBE*)

- admirable (*NIV*)

- excellent (*NIV*)

- praiseworthy

g. If you meditate on these things, and practice the spiritual disciplines taught in the New Testament, what will the result be? (verse 9)

3. What is the only way to change the focus of your mind from this world to the things of God? (Romans 12:2)

   a. How can the Christian best renew his mind?

   b. What will you prove with a renewed mind?

   c. How do you know your own mind is being renewed in the things of God?

DID YOU KNOW?

There is a small verse tucked away in 1 John that explains why we will never find true happiness in this world: "We know that we are of God, and the whole world lies under the sway of the wicked one" (5:19). In other words, there is no contentment for citizens of heaven (Philippians 3:20) to be found in a world where Satan's values prevail. Jesus came into this world to destroy Satan's works and values (1 John 3:8); then it can be recreated and made holy—a new heaven and new earth where God's blessings will be found by those who dwell with Him for eternity (2 Peter 3:10).

Turning Point Resources
by Dr. David Jeremiah

How to Be Happy According to Jesus
The Beatitudes—Matthew 5:1-12

Do money, possessions, success, great accomplishments, fame, and pleasure equal happiness? Jesus' prescription for real joy is exactly the opposite of the world's. Learn about how you can escape Satan's deception that happiness can be bought.

Study Guides HTHSG *(Can-$14/UK-£6)* **$9**
Cassette Album HTHAL (10 tapes) *(Can-$79/UK-£33)* **$50**
Compact Disc Album HTLAL1CD (10 CDs) *(Can-$110/UK-£46)* **$70**

CDs are also available in Spanish
Cómo Ser Feliz Según Jesús HTHALCDS (10 CDs) *(Can-$79/UK-£33)* **$50**

Acts: The Church in Action
The Formation of the Church
Volume 1

The post-Pentecost church in Jerusalem was noted for its power, boldness, and effectiveness—and provides a blueprint for its continuance throughout history. We can learn and apply its principles in the twenty-first century. In volume one of this series, Dr. David Jeremiah shows evidence of its foundational importance to the Christian church today.

Study Guide CIASG1 *(Can - $14/UK-£6)* **$9**
Cassette Album CIAAL1 (12 tapes) *(Can - $95/UK-£39)* **$60**
Compact Disc Album CIAAL1CD (12 CDs) *(Can - $132/UK-£55)* **$84**

Also available on video

ORDER 1-800-947-1993

Turning Point
Resources
by Dr. David Jeremiah

Turning Toward Joy
A Study of Philippians

Written from prison, the apostle Paul's most personal letter was sent to the Christians of Philippi to tell them about the importance of Christian joy. Paul shared that they could experience the joy that Jesus promised those who would follow Him. In this series, Dr. Jeremiah leads you through the book of Philippians so that you, too, can experience the joy of the Lord in your daily life.

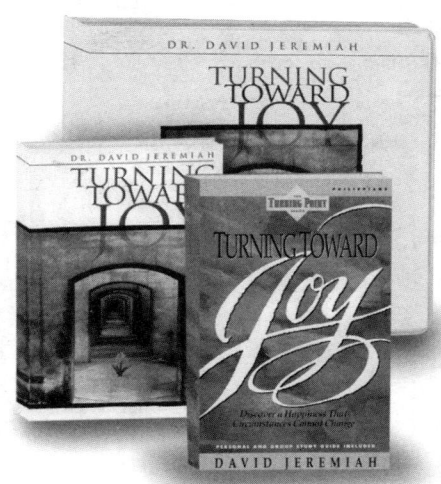

Soft Cover Book TTJBK *Can–$15.75/UK–£6.50)* **$10**
Note: This book contains study materials which are not included in the study guide.

Study Guide TTJSG *(Can–$14/UK–£6)* **$9**
Cassette Album TTJAL (12 tapes) *(Can–$95/UK–£39)* **$60**

Soft cover book and CDs are available in Spanish

Un Giro al Gozo TTJBKS *(Can–$15.75/UK–£6.50)* **$10**
Caminando Hacia el Gozo TTJALS (12 tapes) *(Can–$95/UK–£39)* **$60**

ORDER 1-800-947-1993

Turning Point Resources

STUDY GUIDES
All Study Guides are regularly priced at $9
An audiocassette album is also available for each of the following series.
(Sold separately. Individually priced.)

Acts: The Church in Action (Volume 1)
Authentic Christian Life, The
  (1 Corinthians, 3 Volumes)
Blessings and Behavior of the Believer, The
  (Ephesians, 2 Volumes)
Celebrate His Love (Christmas)
Christians Have Stress Too
Christ's Death and Resurrection
Escape the Coming Night
  (Revelation, 4 Volumes)
Facing the Giants in Your Life
Family Factor
For Such a Time as This (Esther)
Fruit of the Spirit, The (Galatians)
Gifts from God (Parenting)
Giving to God
God in You (The Holy Spirit)
God Meant It for Good (Joseph, 2 Volumes)
Grace of Giving, The (Stewardship)
Greatest Stories Ever Told, The (Parables)
Handwriting on the Wall (Daniel, 3 Volumes)
Heroes of the Faith (Hebrews)
Home Improvement
How to Be Happy According to Jesus
  (The Beatitudes)
How to Live According to Jesus
  (The Sermon on the Mount, 2 Volumes)
Invasion of Other Gods (New Age)
Investing for Eternity
Issues of the Home and Family
Jesus' Final Warning (Prophecy)

Knowing the God You Worship
Learning to Live by Faith (Abraham,
  2 Volumes)
Living by Faith (Romans, 6 Volumes)
Looking for the Savior (Thessalonians,
  2 Volumes)
Miracles of Christ, The
My Heart's Desire (Worship)
Nation in Crisis, A (Joshua, 2 Volumes)
New Spirituality, The (New Age)
Overcoming Loneliness
People God Uses, The
People Who Met Jesus
Power of Encouragement, The
Power of Love, The
Powerful Principles from Proverbs
Prayer—The Great Adventure
Runaway Prophet—Jonah, The
Ruth, Romance, and Redemption
Searching for Heaven on Earth (Ecclesiastes)
Seeking Wisdom—Finding Gold
Signs of the Second Coming
Spiritual Warfare
Stewardship Is Lordship
Ten Burning Questions from Psalms
Tender Warrior, The (David, 2 Volumes)
Turning Toward Integrity (James)
Turning Toward Joy (Philippians)
What the Bible Says About Angels
When Wisdom Turns to Foolishness (Solomon)
When Your World Falls Apart (Psalms)

BOOKS

Escape the Coming Night (Revelation) $13
Gifts from God (Parenting) $19
God in You (The Holy Spirit) $19
Handwriting on the Wall, The (Daniel) $12
Life Wide Open (Purposeful Living) $19
My Heart's Desire (Worship) $19
Power of Encouragement, The $13
Prayer—The Great Adventure $13
Prayer Matrix, The $10
Sanctuary (Daily Devotional) $14

Searching for Heaven on Earth (Ecclesiastes) $22
Slaying the Giants in Your Life $13
Stories of Hope from a Bend in the Road $13
Things That Matter, The $10
Turning Toward Integrity (James) $10
Turning Toward Joy (Philippians) $10
Until I Come (Prophecy) $13
What the Bible Says About Angels $13
When Your World Falls Apart (Psalms) $13

BOOKLETS

Creative Family Living: 20 Ideas for Christian
  Family Interaction $6.50
Family Turning Points $6.50
Financial Turning Points $6.50
How to Encourage Your Children $2.50
Knowing God by Name $2.50
Living Right! 25 Behaviors of a Christian $6.50
Patriotic Turning Points $6.50
Powerful Prayer Promises $2.50

Plan for Whosoever, A $2.50
Prayer for Whosoever, A $2.50
Prophetic Turning Points $6.50
Signs at the Bend in the Road $2.50
Tour of Duty $4.00
Walking Down the Romans Road $2.50
Who I Am in Christ $2.50
Your Greatest Turning Point $2.50

POSTAGE AND HANDLING CHART

For orders	Add
Up to $5.99	$1.50
$6.00-$19.99	$2.50
$20.00-$50.99	$3.50
$51.00-$99.99	$6.00
$100.00 & over	$9.00

If you would like a complete catalog
of resources available from
Turning Point, please call
1-800-947-1993 or write
Turning Point ~ P.O. Box 3838 ~
San Diego, CA 92163-1838.
You can also visit Turning Point at
www.turningpointonline.org